The Romantic Movement

The Romantic Movement

Maurice Cranston

BLACKWELL
Oxford UK & Cambridge USA

First published 1994

Blackwell Publishers
108 Cowley Road
Oxford OX4 1JF
UK

238 Main Street
Cambridge, Massachusetts 02142
USA

British Library Cataloguing in Publication Data
A CIP catalogue record for this book is available from
the British Library.

Library of Congress Cataloging-in-Publication Data
Cranston, Maurice William, 1920–1993
The romantic movement / Maurice Cranston.
p. cm. —
Includes bibliographical references and index.
1. Romanticism. I. Title.
PN603.C73 1994
809′.9145—dc20   93–26713   CIP

ISBN 0–631–17399–4   0 631 194711

Typeset in 12 pt on 14 pt Garamond 3
by Pure Tech Corporation, Pondicherry, India
Printed in Great Britain by
T.J. Press Ltd, Padstow, Cornwall

This book is printed on acid-free paper

Contents

Acknowledgements

This book was written at the Humanities Research Centre in Canberra, and the author is indebted to the Australian National University for the Fellowship which enabled him to spend some months in residence there. He also wishes to express his gratitude to the Suntory-Toyota International Centre and to the Government Research Division of the London School of Economics for financing part of his research.

1

The First Romantics

The romanticism of the Romantic Movement is a product of modernity; it begins in the eighteenth-century Age of Reason, and is in part a reaction against that Age. Historians, whether sympathetic or hostile, are agreed about one thing: Jean-Jacques Rousseau is the first of the Romantics. He introduced the movement – or the 'moment' – in the cultural history of Europe with the publication in 1761 of *La nouvelle Héloïse*, the original romantic novel. Even before that date, however, Rousseau had adumbrated a philosophy of romanticism in his writings on music, in the course of controversy with Jean-Philippe Rameau. The pamphlets with which these two writers battled are nowadays neglected, virtually forgotten, but when they were first published their impact was dramatic. In those pages Rameau outlines a systematic rationalistic theory to justify conservative French aesthetic taste and Rousseau opposes him with an argument for the radical alternative we now call romanticism.

Their controversy was the sequel to the *querelle des Bouffons*, a dispute which had broken out in Paris between supporters of the traditional French opera and supporters of the new Italian opera, the most eloquent champions of Italian music being the young intellectuals attached to the *Encyclopédie* of Diderot and d'Alembert and the defenders of French music being the academic allies of the church and crown. Music in mid-eighteenth-century Paris was still much as it had been in the time of Lully and Louis XIV; it asserted the same Bourbon myths of majesty and *gloire*, proclaiming the splendour of kings, the supremacy of France, and the triumph of order over chaos. At the opera houses, earthly princes were represented on the stage in the image of gods; patriotic sentiments were stirred by the sound of trumpets and drums; and the words, as monotonous as the score, were declaimed with pomp and solemnity. French music spoke to the ear much as the architecture of Versailles addressed the eye.

In the summer of 1752, a company of Italian musicians led by Eustachio Bambini brought to Paris a very different kind of music, works of *opera buffa* by Scarlatti, Leo, Jommelli, Vinci and, first and foremost, Pergolesi. The *Encyclopédistes* promptly made themselves the unpaid publicists of Bambini's troupe. Rousseau, still an active collaborator of the *Encyclopédie*, edited Pergolesi's opera *La serva padrona* for publication in Paris and his then friend, Friedrich Melchior Grimm, wrote a series of pamphlets which argued that French music had become so lifeless, stale and provincial that its only hope lay in reforming itself on the model of the Italian composers who aimed to please rather than elevate the listener, who were satisfied with small orchestras and modest productions, who banished declamation, and whose *libretti* were simple and scored to melodic music of which the *aria*, or song, was the most distinctive feature.

A dozen or more rejoinders to Grimm's pamphlets appeared in print. The main line of their defence of French opera was that it derived from the French dramatic theatre, from the great tradition of Racine and Corneille, which aimed not to amuse but to bear witness to the divine order of the universe; they claimed that French music was, in a word, classical. One thing both sides in the controversy recognized was that the difference between French and Italian opera was not simply a difference between tragedy and comedy; it was a difference between two sorts of music. French music was academic, authoritarian, *élitiste*; Italian music by contrast was natural, spontaneous, popular, and seemed to obey no fixed rules at all. This last was perhaps the secret of its appeal to the *Encyclopédistes*, who, despite all their other disagreements were at one in their yearning for freedom. D'Alembert entered the *querelle des Bouffons* with a pamphlet to which he gave the significant title of *De la liberté de la musique:*

> I am astonished in a century when so many authors busy themselves writing about freedom of trade, freedom of marriage, freedom of the press and freedom in art, that nobody has so far written about freedom in music – for freedom in music entails freedom to feel and freedom to feel means freedom to act, and freedom to act spells the ruin of governments; so let us keep the French opera as it is if we wish to preserve the kingdom, and let us put a brake on singing if we do not want to have liberty in speaking to follow soon afterwards

D'Alembert's pamphlet was attacked as vigorously as Grimm's. His critics demanded to know on what grounds a scientist such as D'Alembert was qualified to pronounce on matters of taste; it was even said to be a betrayal for one of the editors of the *Encyclopédie* to prefer popular music, music fit only to be sung in the streets of Naples or Venice, to classical music; for French music, its supporters protested, was music designed for a cultured audience. And indeed it must be admitted that there was a certain vulgarity in the Italian opera. Even the libretto of *La serva padrona* could be expected to displease a conservative French upper-class public, if that public knew enough Italian to follow it. For Pergolesi's opera is about a maid-servant tricking her bachelor master into marrying her with the happiest of outcomes; it conveys the impertinent message that a maid is as good as a mistress.

What alienated the conservatives was what attracted the liberals. According to an Irish historian, Lady Morgan:

> Paris divided into two musical factions, which were not without their political colours. The privileged class cried out against innovation, even in crochets and quavers, and the noble and the rich, the women and the court clung to the monotonous discords of Lully, Rameau and Mondonville as belonging to the ancient and established order of things, while the musical connoisseurs and amateurs, the men of talent, genius and letters were enthusiastic for nature, taste and Italian music.

Rameau – this was a musician Grimm and d'Alembert and the other critics of French opera had hesitated to criticize. Indeed they considered him to be an intellectual like themselves. D'Alembert in the first volume of the *Encyclopédie* had praised Rameau for being both an outstanding composer and an unrivalled theorist of music. Diderot tried to persuade him to write articles on musical subjects for later volumes of the *Encyclopédie*. Rameau was referred to respectfully as a 'musician–philosopher'. There was, however, something absurd about this posture of the *Encyclopédistes* in attacking French opera while praising the leading French operatic composer, for Rameau had long since taken the place of Lully as the most prolific contributor to the French *théâtre lyrique*. Rameau was also France's leading musicologist and exponent of the principles on which French music was based. His renown was universal, and the *Encyclopédistes* were clearly intimidated by it. And yet it was from their ranks that there emerged a David to challenge this Goliath of aesthetics, Pergolesi's editor Rousseau.

Rousseau attacked Rameau in print as a representative of all that was bad in French music, a composer 'with more knowledge than genius', with 'more cleverness than creativeness', the 'fabricator of over-elaborate counterpoints and harmonies that ought to be relegated to the cloister as their last resting-place'. As for Rameau's theoretical writings, Rousseau went so far as to assert that 'they had acquired their great reputation without ever being actually read'.

There is no mistaking the personal hostility behind these words. Rousseau and Rameau had known each other, and disliked each other, for several years. They had first met in 1745 on decidedly unequal terms. Rameau was then already over sixty years old and at the height of his fame. Rousseau was thirty years younger, an unknown fellow who had come to Paris from Geneva with a project for a new musical notation and the score of an operatic ballet in his pocket. Rousseau's project was politely rejected by the Academy, and when his ballet was given a private performance, Rameau, who was present, rudely and angrily declared it to be a mixture of plagiarism and bad composition. Eight years later Rousseau's situation was much improved. His *Discourse on the Sciences and the Arts* won the essay prize at Dijon, and its publication in Paris was one of the most talked about literary events of 1751. His portrait by Maurice Quinton de La Tour was exhibited at the Paris salon together with those of d'Alembert, Duclos, La Condamine and other leading writers of the time. Moreover Rousseau had established himself almost overnight as an authority on music. He had accepted the job – that Rameau had refused – of writing the articles on musical subjects for the *Encyclopédie* and at Fontainebleau he had enjoyed an enormous fashionable success as a composer with the performance of his opera *Le Devin du village* in which he developed the techniques of Pergolesi into a more lyrical pastoral style. It would be foolish to suggest that Rousseau was as good a musician as Rameau, but the dispute between them soon became a dispute about philosophy, and in that field Rousseau was Rameau's match.

It was a dispute which continued long after Bambini's Italian musicians had left Paris, and although it arose from the *querelle des Bouffons*, Rousseau soon distanced himself from the ideological stance of those *Encyclopédistes* who supported Italian music because it was progressive. He had already made clear in his *Discourse on the Sciences and the Arts* that he had no faith in progress, and although he had already started to write his *Discourse on the Origin of Inequality*, he was no egalitarian. It is instructive to compare the libretto of his *Le Devin du village* with that of Pergolesi's *La serva padrona*. Rousseau's opera introduces a shepherdess who is distressed because her sweetheart has gone off with an aristocratic lady. In the end, love prevails because the village soothsayer helps to restore the shepherd to the shepherdess, and the two are happily and properly united – a very different tale from that of Pergolesi's opera, where a servant is shown to be the right bride for the master. If the message of *La serva padrona* is egalitarian, the argument of Rousseau's opera is that people should find love and happiness in their own station in society, and not try to trespass across the barriers of class.

It is hardly astonishing that *Le Devin du village* should have given such pleasure to the King at Fontainebleau, for however 'radical' the music, the libretto is plainly conservative, and although the King felt duty-bound to protect French music against Italian competition, he could hardly conceal the fact that he personally enjoyed Rousseau's Italian-style music more than that of the French composers. Indeed, after the success of *Le Devin du village* Rousseau could have received a royal pension if only he had had the grace to pay his respects to the King. He had decided, however, to resist all temptations of worldly glory as a musician in order to preserve his integrity as a philosopher; and it was as a philosopher that he resumed his attack on the principles of Rameau.

Rameau's first instinct was to ignore the impudent Swiss upstart, but with Rousseau installed as chief musicologist of the *Encyclopédie*, he realized he could no longer afford to do so. As a result, it was not only Rousseau himself who stopped composing music to write about the theory of music, Rameau was forced to do the same. In the following years he produced a succession of books and pamphlets including: *Observations sur notre instinct pour la musique, Erreurs sur la musique dans l'Encyclopédie, Réponse aux éditeurs de l'Encyclopédie* and *Code de la musique pratique*.

Rousseau, on his side, brought out, together with numerous articles, an equally long series of separate works: *Lettre sur la musique française, Dissertation sur la musique moderne, Lettre à Monsieur Raynal, Examen des deux principes avancés par Monsieur Rameau* and his *Dictionnaire de musique*. This is the earliest theoretical literature of romanticism.

Rameau took very seriously the role of a philosopher of music. He argued that the purpose of music was not simply to please the ear, but to give us knowledge of reality. Scientists had explained that the universe was a systematic whole, intelligible to reason. The purpose of music was to provide, through the testimony of hearing, a 'double confirmation' of the rational order of creation. 'When we think', he wrote, 'of the infinite relations that the fine arts have to one another, and to the sciences, it is only logical to conclude that they are governed by one and the same principle. That principle is harmony'. Rameau went even further in his claims for harmony. It was not only the central principle of music, it was the basic principle of all the arts. Moreover, since harmony was more readily discernible in music than in any other form, music should be recognized as 'the first of the arts'.

Rousseau agreed that music was the first of the arts, but he asserted that its ruling principle was not harmony but melody. It was only because music could do more than any other art, he suggested, that it was entitled to priority:

Music can depict things we cannot hear, while it is impossible for the painter to paint things we cannot see; and it is the great genius of an art which acts only by movement, to use movement even to provide the image of repose. Slumber, the calm of night, solitude, even silence are among the scenes that music can depict. Sometimes sound produces the effect of silence, sometimes silence the effect of sound, just as a man dozes during a steady monotonous reading and then awakens, startled, when the reading ceases. It is the same with other effects . . . the art of the musician consists in substituting for the invisible image of the object, that of the movements which its presence excites in the mind of the spectator . . . Not only does the musician move the waves of the sea at will, fan the flames of a fire, make streams flow, rain fall and torrents rush down, he can magnify the horror of a burning desert, darken the walls of a dungeon, or he can calm a storm, soften the air and lighten the sky, and spread, with his orchestra, a fresh breeze through the woods.

Reality for Rousseau is visible palpable nature; and music, he says, can conjure up that nature. It can also express human feeling which is nature, so to speak, within us; and the expression of feeling, he claims, is achieved through melody. Thus, when Rousseau and Rameau quarrelled over melody and harmony they were concerned with something more than music; their dispute was about reality itself. For Rameau, reality was the Newtonian universe accessible to reason; for Rousseau it was the concrete world of perception and experience.

Where Rameau, in his Cartesian manner, demanded unity, Rousseau was content with variety; where Rameau looked for fixed rules in music as in mathematics, Rousseau insisted that music was logically different from mathematics, and that musical styles must vary as nature varied. It was the marvellous gift of melody that it could express what was natural, whereas harmony was essentially artificial, an invention of the mind.

Rameau insisted that anyone who thought melody prior to harmony did not recognize the true character of music. To deny harmony was to repudiate all those sciences which were based on the same mathematical principles of proportion and progression. Melody, he agreed, was an important part of music, but he argued that it was generated by the harmonic arrangement of sounds. Hence the man who understood only melody understood very little about music, while the man who had mastered harmony understood almost everything. Music, Rameau declared, must be seen to be at the same time an art and a science. The laws of music and laws of geometry rested on the same foundations. Indeed, music could claim to be the first of the sciences for the same reasons that made it the first of the arts.

Rousseau clung equally tenaciously to his belief in the priority of melody. Thus we find him, for example, in the article on *mélodie* in his *Dictionnaire de musique* arguing that whereas harmony serves a subordinate purpose in holding the different parts of a musical composition together, melody provides the force and energy and the flow of music. While harmony may speak to the ear, melody speaks to the heart.

Rousseau made many enemies when he developed his attack on Rameau's theory into an attack on French music in general, based on the notion that French was an unmusical language of northern origin that could not easily be sung, in contrast to Italian which was southern and musical. As a result of his saying this in his *Lettre sur la musique française* all the agitation provoked by earlier pamphleteering in the *querelle des Bouffons* came to be centred on Rousseau himself. His *Confessions* contained a passage which has puzzled many readers:

> In 1753 the *parlement* of Paris had just been exiled by the King; unrest was at its height; all the signs pointed to an early uprising. My *Lettre sur la musique française*

appeared, and all other quarrels were immediately forgotten. No one thought of anything but the danger to
French music, and the only uprising that took place was
against me. The battle was so fierce that the nation was
never to recover from it . . . If I say that my writings
may have averted a political revolution in France, people
will think me mad; nevertheless it is a very real truth.

Is it conceivable that a musical dispute could have diverted
aggression that would otherwise have gone into a political
revolt? Others besides Rousseau believed it. Mercier, in his
Tableau de Paris writes: 'Ah, how the Government ought to
cherish the opera! The theatrical factions made all the other
factions disappear'. Grimm reported in his *Correspondance lit-
téraire* that the public was 'much more interested in the
quarrel provoked by Rousseau's *Lettre* than in the Royal
Chamber and its affairs'. Cultural questions were taken seriously in mid-eighteenth-century Paris, and Rousseau's attack
on French music put many people into a frenzy of anger.

Rousseau felt himself to be persecuted, even as Rameau felt
himself to be betrayed by the *Encyclopédistes* who refused to
accept his theory of the superiority of harmony over melody.
But in a very important sense Rousseau had succeeded where
Rameau had failed. Rousseau had propelled French music
into a new direction, away from the artificial constraints of
the seventeenth century towards the creative freedom of the
future. By the example of his *Le Devin du village* and his
doctrine of the supremacy of melody over harmony he had
introduced a new development in the history of western
culture. On the musical stage he prepared the way for Mozart,
whose *Bastien und Bastienne* is based on *Le Devin du village*, and
for the operas of Gluck, who brought new life to the French
opera after the death of Rameau. Gluck once wrote:

All I have tried to accomplish as a musician is to produce
the kind of work which Jean-Jacques Rousseau would

have produced if he had not forsaken composition in
order to write books.

Gluck and his successors developed as composers the full
potentialities of romantic music envisaged in Rousseau's
theory; Rousseau himself went on to produce a model of totally
romantic art in another medium, that of literature, with his
novel *La nouvelle Héloïse*. Its appearance in 1761 turned Rousseau from a celebrity into the object of a cult. *La nouvelle
Héloïse* was a universal best seller, devoured by readers, and
not least by the ladies of fashion about whom Rousseau had
written many ungracious words. Julie, the heroine of *La
nouvelle Héloïse*, was hailed as a perfect woman; and Rousseau
received a constant flow of letters asking for more informa-
tion about her and even for her portrait. As for Julie's lover,
women readers yearned to meet him. The message of the
novel was seen as a liberating one: that the imagination need
no longer be the slave of reason, that feelings should not be
suppressed, denied in the name of decorum; that if only one
could strip away the falseness and pretence by which modern
society was dominated, there was goodness to be discovered
in the human heart.

La nouvelle Héloïse changed lives and fashions. Buffon once
said: 'Others write, but Monsieur Rousseau commands.' The
romanticism which was adumbrated in his theories of music
was now exemplified in Rousseau's imaginary persons, and
French readers were so thrilled by what they saw that they
began to forsake the rigid mores of a neo-classical, Gallican
and Cartesian tradition to think and feel in new ways. The
Enlightenment had already poured scorn on religion and
traditional political beliefs, but its Baconian empiricism was
too dry and utilitarian to offer a satisfying alternative to
Catholic spirituality. Rousseau's romanticism, by contrast,
was rich enough in emotional intensity to replace lost faith
with new excitements.

The form Rousseau chose for his novel was one which Richardson and others had made popular in the eighteenth century – the *roman épistolaire*, a series of letters in which fiction could be given the appearance of fact. Rousseau presented himself to the public not as the author but as the 'editor' of the letters in the book, and even carried this platonic 'noble lie' to the point of assuring his friends that he had discovered what were described in the original title as *Lettres de deux amants*. However contrived this procedure, the aim was to achieve the effect of authenticity as opposed to the manifest artificiality of neo-classical literature. Rousseau's fiction was dressed up as fact to serve, like melody in music, as 'the true voice of feeling', to communicate an understanding of human experience in all its immediacy and intensity.

Rousseau also intended *La nouvelle Héloïse* to be a moral tale, and he was particularly gratified when readers recognized it as such, for not all readers did. The novel does not preach conventional morality as does, for example, Richardson's *Pamela* which had been highly esteemed in France since its appearance in 1740. Richardson's heroine is a girl who cherishes her virginity as a capital which she will exchange for nothing less than a marriage contract, a bargain she triumphantly effects after many trials and temptations. *Pamela* provides a lesson in bourgeois prudence. *La nouvelle Héloïse* is a moral tale in a very different sense. The central conflict of the story is not between reason and passion, for it is one principle of the romanticism which Rousseau introduced that human beings are not governed by reason: the conflict in *La nouvelle Héloïse* is between one passion and another. Rousseau's ideal woman – Julie – is the daughter of a Vaudois baron who employs as her tutor a young man of bourgeois origins named St-Preux. St-Preux falls in love with Julie and she with him, she encourages him to make love to her and promises to be his for ever. Her father, however, is horrified at the idea of his daughter marrying a bourgeois and tells his

daughter that she must marry into her own class and to a man
of his choosing. The chosen bridegroom is an upright and
coolly estimable atheist, the Baron de Wolmar. Julie, who
adores her father and dreads the consequences of breaking his
heart, asks St-Preux to release her from her pledge. St-Preux
nobly acquiesces; and Julie goes on to atone for her youthful
misdemeanour by becoming in Wolmar's model feudal household the perfect Christian wife and mother. Some years later
St-Preux returns from a wandering life to the Wolmars' estate
at Clarens on the shores of Lake Geneva as tutor to their
children; but as he goes on excursions with Julie around the
lake against a backdrop of alpine scenery it becomes agoniz-
ingly clear that she has never ceased to love him and death
itself has to intervene to keep her from returning once more
to his arms.

In correspondence with readers of the novel, Rousseau explained clearly that Julie's motive for rejecting St-Preux was
not one of duty, but of love for her father, who would, she
believed, die if she disobeyed him. To a friend who protested
that Julie was doubly unfaithful in first repudiating her
pledge to St-Preux and then marrying a man she did not love,
Rousseau argued that the novelist's task was not to show
people acting as they ought to act (as conventional novelists
such as Richardson might choose to do) but to show people
acting according to their character as they would act in real
life. The novelist should be a truthful chronicler of human
behaviour.

Rousseau's belief that such human behaviour is governed
by passion rather than reason was not new. Pascal had asserted no less in his critique of Cartesian rationalism, but
Pascal was a pious Jansenist, to whom the self, *le moi*, was
hateful, whereas to Rousseau, and the Romantics who came
after him, the self was the object of the highest and most
enduring interest. Many readers assumed that St-Preux was
based on the author himself; Voltaire declared that the novel

was nothing other than Rousseau's autobiography. But in so far as *La nouvelle Héloïse* is autobiographical, it is only indirectly so. Some years later Rousseau produced a book that was directly autobiographical, autobiographical to an extent unprecedented in European literature: the *Confessions*, in which he declared his purpose to be to unveil the truth about one man's experience of life as candidly as no author had ever done before. He took the title of the book from St Augustine, but whereas the Saint's *Confessions* were addressed from a penitent to God, Rousseau's *Confessions* were written without repentance, as an exercise at once in self-justification and self-display. All the restraint demanded by traditional culture was thrown to the winds as Rousseau stripped bare his soul and his past. His autobiography was an innovation in literature, no less revolutionary than *La nouvelle Héloïse*; the novel introduced serious romantic fiction to French literature, the *Confessions* introduced the romantic personality: Jean-Jacques himself, the virtuous exemplar. While he asserted his individuality and uniqueness, he also claimed to be somehow representative of everyone. Rousseau believed that all members of the human race had, at the deepest level, some things in common. He once told his beloved Sophie d'Houdetot that he could learn about her soul by looking into his own. He discovered the secrets of humanity by means of introspection.

His attachment to Sophie was itself one of the outcomes of *La nouvelle Héloïse*. Having created his ideal woman – Julie – in imagination, Rousseau afterwards recognized her in reality in the person of the Comtesse d'Houdetot, who encouraged him to flirt with her and with whom he fell in love. Alas, his affair with her proved no more enduring than St-Preux's affair with Julie. After a summer in Rousseau's arms, Sophie rejected him in favour of the Marquis de St-Lambert just as Julie had rejected St-Preux in favour of the Baron de Wolmar. Nature imitated art.

In the *Confessions* Rousseau recalls Sophie saying to him 'No lover loved as you loved'; in the novel St-Preux tells Julie that, for him, love is an all-consuming feeling – it is his life. Romantic love surpasses the sexual, not by sublimating it in the platonic manner, but by assimilating the sexual to a total passion which is as much metaphysical as physical, and which tends to be intensified rather than modified by frustration. At the same time Rousseau suggests that love purifies sexual congress and carries it into an altogether different realm from that of lust.

In any case, Rousseau's romanticism does not judge in terms of rules and precepts. It has much in common with the morality of earlier German pietists, who argued that the Christian life should be guided by Christ's example of charity in all things rather than by adherence to a code of Old Testament commandments and interdictions. Rousseau himself made the acquaintance of German pietism through his first mistress Mme de Warens, who did much to educate him when he lived with her in his later adolescence. Although she converted to Catholicism after she left Switzerland, Mme de Warens had herself been educated by a Swiss adherent of German pietism, François Magny, and absorbed much of his teaching. If she did not live according to conventional rules of chastity and thrift, she felt that she was a better Christian for always following the impulses of a generous heart.

Pietism also authorized what Pascal forbade, the contemplation of the self, albeit the self understood as the soul. But for pietism to be developed into romanticism, it had to be purged of its Lutheran obsession with salvation and the doctrine of original sin, and to recognize the soul as a thing of beauty. This Rousseau, with his supreme assurance of the purity of his own soul, felt well placed to accomplish. His religious creed was minimal: belief in the benevolence of Providence and in life after death was all that remained of Christianity in his system. But to that minimum he clung with a humble and reverent devotion.

He had the temperament of a worshipper, and the object of that worship was one which was to take the place of God for many later Romantics, and which he himself identified with God, namely nature – nature in those forms least touched by the hand of man, high mountains and deep forests and wind-swept lakes. In the alpine scenery of Switzerland, St-Preux comes close to having a mystical experience, and it is against a background of the rocks and gorges of the southern shore of Lake Geneva, where St-Preux and Julie are trapped by a storm, that their love comes closest to overcoming their moral scruples. The Alps, an object of horror for the Age of Reason, became for Romantics of the generations that fol-lowed Rousseau, a place of pilgrimage. People lost the taste for formal gardens and artificial lakes, favouring instead na-ture, as Rousseau had described it, in its wildest and most savage forms. He taught his readers to see the world with new eyes.

This element of romanticism was to prove a source of inspiration and renewal in painting. For Fragonard, Watteau, Boucher, Chardin and the other leading painters of the age of Louis XV, nature was domesticated nature: orchards, meadows, gardens and elegant *fêtes champêtres*; from Fuseli to Courbet, nature was represented as Rousseau had seen it, although fully romantic painting took longer to manifest itself than romantic literature, if only because revolutionary France favoured neo-classical art in its attempt to restore the ideals of ancient Rome.

Romantics who came after Rousseau sought inspiration in the arts and life-styles of the Middle Ages, but he himself had no share in this. Although he was profoundly critical of modernity, he always insisted that there was no going back in time either to the state of nature he described in his political writings or to the period of nascent society he called the golden age of humanity. The only escape from the sophist-icated modern world he envisaged was an escape into villages and country places which had not been corrupted by the industries and luxuries and cultural institutions of cities. This is another aspect of his cult of nature: the retreat to rusticity.

Rousseau claimed to be a Christian, indeed a better Christian than most adherents of established churches, but Christ was not seen by him as the Redeemer, nor even as the object of adoration and prayer. Christ was rather a being in whom he saw himself prefigured, a good man ill used, a victim of society's hostility. St-Preux who loses Julie to Wolmar, is hardly the hero of *La nouvelle Héloïse*, and Rousseau himself, chased from one refuge to another, vilified and mocked, depicts himself in the *Confessions* as another loser. Even so, he establishes for such victims a place in romantic mythology as compelling as that of the hero. After St-Preux comes the Werther of Goethe, the René of Chateaubriand and all the wounded and defeated warriors who figure in the paintings of Géricault. Romanticism was to have its heroes, its conquerors, even as classicism had; but what is distinctive is the 'anti-hero', the victim, the man of sorrows like Rousseau himself. Poets, claimed a later Romantic, Shelley, are

> cradled into poetry by wrong;
> They learn in suffering what they teach in song . . .

If Rousseau was the first philosopher of romanticism, he was not the only one, even among the *Encyclopédistes*, to make an important contribution to its formulation. There was also Diderot, his contemporary, the great friend with whom he quarrelled, but with whom his ideas continued often to coincide. Diderot had taken Rousseau's side in the controversy with Rameau; and felt as Rousseau felt about the primacy of imagination over reason. Baconian as Diderot was in his faith in progress and the belief that science and technology could be the salvation of mankind, he rejected Bacon's empiricist conception of science as an exercise in observation and induction. On the contrary, Diderot argued that science was primarily an activity of imagination and conjecture.

The element of imagination in science Diderot spoke of as 'l'esprit de divination' or the capacity to 'sniff out' hidden connections between things by the pursuit of vague ideas, suspicions, hints and even fantasies 'which the mind when excited takes for accurate pictures'. The true scientist, for Diderot, was not essentially different from the artist; both required 'a delicate awareness' of things seen and both required intuition. 'Nature', he wrote, 'is like a woman who enjoys disguising herself, and whose different disguises, revealing now one part of her and now another, permit those who study her assiduously to hope that one day they may know the whole of her person.'

The sciences which interested Diderot most were not those which informed the rationalism of Newton and his successors: astronomy and physics, where nature was perceived in its most orderly and regular movements, and explained in the bloodless categories of mathematics. Diderot's sciences were the biological sciences which studied the far less readily predictable movements of living things, sciences which observed nature in a state of constant flux. 'Who knows what species of animals preceded us? And who knows what species of animals will follow ours? Everything changes, everything passes.' Whereas the Newtonian scientists found reassuring models of nature's laws in the movements of the planets, Diderot claimed that the study of 'monsters' such as Siamese twins is what can give access to nature's secrets. By such suggestions Diderot propelled even scientific minds away from rationalism and towards romanticism.

He contributed no less to the romantic conception of freedom, which he visualized as something akin to John Stuart Mill's notion of liberty as 'self-realization'. Diderot asserted this most forcefully in his *Réfutation* of Helvétius. That celebrated *philosophe* had argued, as a thoroughgoing rationalist, that all human beings are virtually identical in construction so that by the right training and motivation anyone could be made to do anything that anyone else could do. Diderot argued against this that the variety of human achievements not only showed that men had different upbringings and lived in different environments, but that they possessed different inherent natures; each individual was unique.

Diderot went beyond the mere observation of such differences to attach great value to them. Like Mill after him, he had the highest admiration for people who cultivated their own originality. He said it was from the ranks of *les originaux* that men of genius sprang, and that men of genius were the salt of the earth. He was even attracted by wicked men, and wrote with pleasure about them in such books as *La religieuse* and *Jacques le fataliste* to illustrate the enthralling diversity of human personalities.

One of the reasons why Diderot admired 'originals' was that they achieved that freedom which is 'self-realization', the uninhibited expression of a man's own individuality. Such freedom was by no means universally enjoyed and Diderot did not think it was within everyone's capacity. He simply thought that people who achieved it were the most interesting, and he had a low opinion of those who gave up the pursuit of it for the sake of a dull comfortable conformist life: 'I hate all those sordid little things that reveal only an abject soul, but I do not hate great crimes, first because beautiful paintings and great tragedies are made out of them, and secondly because noble and sublime deeds share with great crimes the same quality of energy.'

When Diderot speaks like this, we hear already the authentic voice of romanticism. Moreover, with his ideal of the 'genius' Diderot bequeathed to romanticism an object of veneration that is not to be found in Rousseau. After Diderot's death, Kant gave the ideal an added clarity by distinguishing sharply between genius and talent, the accomplishments of

2

German Romanticism

Romanticism is often said to have been a 'reaction against classicism'. In Germany it was a reaction rather against rationalism, emerging together with a new kind of classicism in the glorious flowering of literature that took place in the eighteenth century. Rousseau had his most ardent readers in Germany, and historians have suggested several reasons for this, although his success is hardly bewildering in view of the fact that in finding inspiration in seventeenth-century Lutheran pietism, Rousseau had drawn from a German source.

The Germans of Rousseau's time were living between two worlds; they had left the feudal past, but they had not been propelled into modernity, like the French, by absolutism or, like the English and the Dutch, by revolutions. Their so-called Holy Roman Empire remained intact as a loose confederation of some three hundred principalities, each virtually autonomous, and all more or less aristocratic in their social structure. Wars and religious upheavals had introduced change without progress. The diversity of petty rulers meant that the Germans had experience of both good government and bad, and learned the habits of endurance: a conservative and contemplative people. The greatest break with the past, the Protestant Reformation, had served to set Germans at war with one another, and ended with Germany divided between

Catholic and Protestant princes. No longer held together under the effective sovereignty of a single emperor, or by the authority of a universal church, Germany in the eighteenth century was without any real political or institutional identity; Germany, said Voltaire, was just a word, a geographical expression.

From the point of view of the Enlightenment this did not matter. The Enlightenment believed in the unity of all humanity, the universal rights of men, and the uniformity, if not equality, of all rational beings. Superior minds in eighteenth-century Germany – Kant, for example, Lessing, Lichtenberg, Christian Wolff and Moses Mendelssohn – welcomed the Enlightenment and made it their own as the *Aufklärung*; but the greatest philosopher among them, Kant, was widely thought to have demolished reason when he denied the possibility of knowledge of things in themselves. Moreover, the German Protestant clergy, for all the high scholarship of their universities, were hardly more sympathetic to the Enlightenment than were the Catholics. Indeed they were perhaps more alarmed by it, as they discovered that their own arguments against the Catholic religion could serve equally as arguments against Protestant beliefs. The Lutheran church, in making every man a priest unto himself, had surrendered the clergy's right to authority in the interpretation of the scriptures. Leaving that duty to Everyman's reason, it had activated an untrustworthy instrument.

Hence the retreat from reason of the seventeenth-century pietists, who based their faith on love of Christ as distinct from intellectual adherence to a creed; and hence in the eighteenth century the eager reception of romanticism in a Germany awakened but not persuaded by the critical rationalism of the Enlightenment. We cannot be surprised that the first theorist to incorporate Rousseau's ideas into German philosophy should have been a Lutheran pastor, Johann Gottfried Herder. After reading *Émile*, Herder came to the conclusion that religion had no need for reason; it could be reconstructed on a basis of feeling. He went on to develop a system in which sensibility took the place of rational persuasion, claiming that knowledge of God could be attained through a consciousness of oneness with the whole – the whole meaning nature, history and all the works of man as well as the divine being. From this exercise in theology, Herder went on to elaborate theories of history and of language which were even more important in the formation of German romantic thought. He depicted history as an evolutionary process with laws of its own analogous to those of nature, a process in which, by stages, men struggled within their diverse cultures and language groups, towards the ultimate fulfilment of all the potentialities of humanity. In the light of this theory, Germany could no longer be brushed aside as 'a geographical expression'; it was a community united by a shared history and the common language of its members, a cultural family writ large.

Herder was not satisfied with theoretical exposition; he published what was in effect a call to action to the poets and artists and scholars of Germany to enlarge the consciousness of their people by new creations in their national idiom and by recovering the half-forgotten artistic achievements of the German past. In his book on the *Origin of Languages* first published in 1772, Herder made exalted claims for language, describing it as the faculty which distinguished human beings from beasts, and elaborating Rousseau's notion that man's first language was poetry, and saying of poetry what Rousseau said of music – that it was the true voice of feeling. Language was more important than music for Herder, for whereas music is an almost universal art, languages belong to separate societies and to man's experience 'as a creature of the herd'.

German authors in Herder's time were only just beginning to exploit the full riches of the German language. Philosophers such as Leibniz had written in Latin; Frederick the Great encouraged the use of French; Lessing, who subscribed to the

Enlightenment ideal of a universal culture, wrote works in German based on neo-classical models which were all French. Herder protested that this adherence to the canons of French taste was a form of constraint. The French language, moulded by Cartesians, bound French writers to the principles implicit in it; but German authors, thinking and writing in German, had no such impediment to an appreciation of other literatures, such as English, Spanish or Italian. Herder, a true cosmopolitan despite his national mission, helped the Germans recognize the merits of Shakespeare, Cervantes and other great writers, who were ignored in France. He also followed Rousseau in asserting the value of popular, demotic or folkloric poetry, which he offered as proof that German literature had its own history. He edited a two-volume collection of *Volkslieder*, not all German in origin, but translated into German to reinforce his efforts to secure recognition for Germany's place in Europe's cultural heritage.

At Strasbourg in the year 1771, Herder acquired an unlikely convert to his ideas in the person of the young Goethe – unlikely because Goethe had established his reputation as the author of lyrics in the rococo mode and of plays written in alexandrines under the influence of Racine. However, Herder opened his eyes to the liberating possibilities of the Shakespearean form of drama and Goethe went on to write a historical play animated by all the fire and fury of *Macbeth*, with a sixteenth-century German knight as its central protagonist, *Götz von Berlichingen*. This marked the introduction into German literature of *Sturm und Drang*, the first period of German romanticism. It took its name from the title of a play by Friedrich Maximilian Klinger, who wrote a series of *Ritterdrama* inspired by *Götz von Berlichingen* and informed by his experience as an officer in the Russian army.

Goethe himself moved in his next important work from the Shakespearean model to a more domestic scene, and produced a novel, *Die Leiden des jungen Werthers*, which is romantic in a totally Rousseauesque sense. It was first published in 1774, thirteen years after *La nouvelle Héloïse*; it, too, is an epistolary novel, although there is no exchange of correspondence, only a series of letters written to a friend by the central figure, Werther, together with a commentary by the author posing as the editor. *Werther* is shorter than Rousseau's novel, but has the same cast of three: Werther, the young lover, who is like St-Preux; Lotte, the loved one, a somewhat diminished version of Rousseau's Julie; and Lotte's husband, Albert, very much another Wolmar. The plot in both novels is similar. Werther, a young man of acute sensibility, is sent on a matter of family business to a small German town where life is simple, society is patriarchal and the countryside is close at hand. Werther is enchanted by everything, especially by nature as he wanders in the fields and woods: 'A marvellous serenity', he writes, 'has taken possession of my whole soul, like the sweet spring mornings.' His serenity, however, is disturbed when he meets a girl named Lotte and falls in love with her. Unfortunately for Werther, Lotte is already engaged to the estimable Albert. Werther, as he himself puts it 'cannot understand how someone else can – may – love her, given that I alone love her, so fully, so intensely, and know nothing else.' Lotte encourages Werther's flirtation, but makes him understand that she will marry Albert. Unable to endure the frustration, Werther goes to the capital of the principality and finds a government job, only to be humiliated by his aristocratic employers; for Werther, like St-Preux, is a mere bourgeois, and must be punished for it. Eventually Werther returns to Lotte's little town. Although Lotte has by this time married Albert, she welcomes Werther's attentions, and Albert seems to tolerate their friendship and constant meetings. As a result, the 'editor' informs us, 'Werther became so precious to Lotte that she shared everything she thought or felt with him.' Werther kisses her chastely, and reads to her from poetry, first Homer then Ossian.

Torn between her attachment to her model husband and
the emotions she feels in the presence of Werther, Lotte
becomes agitated and Albert less patient: 'Against her will
she felt deep in her heart the ardour of Werther's embraces,
and at once the days of unclouded innocence ended.' Werther,
realizing that his love for Lotte is hopeless, borrows a pair of
pistols from Albert and shoots himself.

The popular success of Goethe's *Werther* exceeded even that
of *La nouvelle Héloïse*, and continued for many years throughout
Europe; the French composer, Massenet, made an opera out of
Werther in 1892. In the eighteenth century, Goethe's novel
became, like *La nouvelle Héloïse*, the object of a cult. Numerous lovesick young men imitated Werther and shot themselves; more took to wearing Werther's costume of blue and
yellow.

Goethe himself became half-embarrassed by the book, although he rewrote it in the 1780s for a new edition. He felt
it was too autobiographical. Just as Rousseau admitted putting himself into St-Preux, Goethe said 'Werther has much
in common with me'; he also said 'the author of *Werther* did
the wrong thing in not shooting himself once he had finished
writing it.' What Goethe actually did was curb in himself the
wild tendencies that Herder had urged him to let free. He
came afterwards to speak of the classical as the healthy and
the romantic as the morbid. He once drew attention to the
point that Werther's decline from sanity into suicidal madness could be dated from his turning from reading Homer to
Lotte to reading Ossian.

Ossian, the non-existent early Gaelic poet invented in the
1770s by James Macpherson, was a favourite of Herder's. And
just as Macpherson in pretending that the Ossian poems were
genuine was prompted by the desire to assert the cultural
superiority of the Celts to their English conquerors, so Herder in promoting Ossian, had a similar motive: to demon-
strate the superiority of the primitive, the earthy, the

spontaneous and folkloric in art over the products of sophisticated French taste. Ossian had the added advantage from
Herder's point of view of being 'northern', which meant that
he could be captured together with the newly translated sagas
from Iceland and Scandinavia in Herder's wide net of the
Germanic.

Ossian, the Celt, thus became the subject of the essay
Herder wrote for what was seen as the manifesto of *Sturm und
Drang*, a collection entitled *Von deutschen Art und Kunst*, to
which Goethe contributed an essay in praise of Gothic architecture. From the ideological perspective, perhaps the most
significant contribution to the manifesto was Justus Möser's
on German history, for it adumbrates the conception – so
important for later romanticism – of the German nation as
a people evolving towards full political union in a single
state.

Von deutschen Art und Kunst was published in 1773. Nine
years later there was staged at Mannheim what is often named
as the perfect model of a *Sturm und Drang* drama, *Die Räuber*
by J. C. F. Schiller. This could easily seem to be a romantic
play, taking its cue from a plea of Diderot's to present the
criminal as hero. But it asks to be understood as a classical
play, and was seen as such by Goethe, who by the 1780s had
distanced himself from the romantic tendency he had encouraged in others.

Die Räuber is a play about freedom in which the romantic
pursuit of freedom as self-realization or self-fulfilment is
shown to be a doomed enterprise. Schiller's claim to be a
classical dramatist rests on his central purpose, which is to
write authentic tragedies in the great European tradition,
where a metaphysical framework is a necessary part of the
tragic vision. Whereas the gods preside over a divinely ordered universe for the Greeks, and a single God provides the
universal sanction for the Christian dramatists, the moral law
itself is elevated to the status of a metaphysical power in

Schiller, and this is what makes it logically possible for him to write tragedies. A purely romantic dramatist, who makes a god of man, can give no meaning to tragedy. At the end of *Die Räuber*, the criminal–hero kills himself 'to appease the law he has offended and restore order to the world'. It is this ability to place his characters in a moral world above the human which separates Schiller, philosophically, from his romantic contemporaries.

Both Goethe and Schiller are classical writers in another sense, that of rising above the prevailing level of literary achievement to provide timeless models of excellent normality. Schiller's achievement was to prolong the life of tragedy after the death of God. Goethe was a post-Renaissance polymath – poet, philosopher, scientist, dramatist, novelist, statesman, moralist and sage – who assimilated his early romanticism into a monumental *oeuvre* which transcends all the familiar categories. Goethe's Faust protests:

> *Grau . . . ist alle Theorie*
> *Und grün des Lebens goldener Baum.*

German romanticism, however, was impregnated with theory. After Herder came Johann Gottlieb Fichte, who was appointed to the chair of philosophy at Jena in 1794 at the age of thirty-two. His starting point was Kant's thesis that the mind, having no knowledge of things in themselves, imposes its own categories of order on the external world in order to understand it. Whereas Kant stressed the rational nature of the categories which the mind had to impose on the world, Fichte stressed the isolation, the independence, and supremacy of each man's mind or, as he preferred to call it, the ego or the self. And where Kant worked inward from the concept of the world to discover the role of the individual mind, Fichte works from the mind outwards to argue that the world is a product of the ego; he divides the whole of reality into the ego and the non-ego. On the one side, here am I; out there is the external world constructed by my creative imagination. It was such arguments, first putting the imagination in the place of reason and then asserting the sovereignty of the self or ego that made Fichte so important a philosopher in the history of romanticism.

When Kant denied the possibility of knowledge of things in themselves, he did not deny their existence. Fichte did. He made the external world wholly dependent on the subjective observer. Objective reality, or the non-ego, is constructed by the ego as its own limiting and therefore delimiting opposite. The ego is constantly active, creating the world as it reaches out in thought towards the infinite. The universe exists as an idea in the mind of the beholder.

The writers and artists of German romanticism found in Fichte's theory a justification for the interest they took in their own egos; an interest an earlier generation would have condemned as narcissism. What Rousseau and *Werther* made fashionable, Fichte made respectable, even noble. For while he seemed to deny access to objective truth, he recognized man's yearning for what surpasses the limits of his perception, an 'impulse towards something entirely unknown which reveals itself only in the sense of need for it, in a dissatisfaction or emptiness which knows not how it might be satisfied'. Fichte considered this yearning to be wholesome, since it expressed that striving which was necessary to the ego's function of creating reality. The pursuit of the absolute, Fichte suggested, is what unites the philosopher and the poet.

Several poets came under Fichte's influence when he taught at the University of Jena; and Jena, in effect, became the centre of that group of writers who introduced the word *Romantik* into the German language. They published a literary revue *Die Athenaeum*, and generally dedicated themselves both to the theory and the practice of the ideals that Fichte had elaborated. The group, which came to be known as the *Jenaer Kreis*, included Friedrich Schlegel, his elder brother

August Wilhelm Schlegel, Friedrich von Hardenberg, who wrote under the name Novalis, and Johann Ludwig Tieck.

Friedrich Schlegel was perhaps the most influential figure among them if only as a literary critic; he provided romanticism with its aesthetics. In his earliest writings Schlegel reiterated classical principles, proclaiming his respect for the law of unities, and other rules laid down by Aristotle for the judgement of a literary genre. He attempted to modernize Aristotle by arguing that beauty has three constituents: unity, multiplicity and totality; and he went on to extend these concepts to take in a good deal that classical taste would have rejected, but his project of modernizing Aristotle eventually collapsed in the face of Fichte's refutation of objective universals. Herder had already convinced Schlegel that there were no universal literary genres on the grounds that each genre is relative to its own changing culture. Fichte persuaded him that there were no fixed laws in art and that aesthetic judgements could be neither demonstrated nor proved.

Schlegel did not shrink from the implications of these beliefs. Classical aesthetics would have to be abandoned. The task of the literary critic was still to judge; but somehow he must judge without rules to guide him. How was this to be done? Could romanticism produce a critical theory to replace that of classicism? Schlegel suggested that it could: in the absence of universal principles, he argued that every single work of art could be judged by the principles it incorporated in itself. It would be the function of the critic first to investigate a given work so as to ascertain what ideal it sought to achieve and then to judge how far it satisfied that ideal.

Schlegel admitted that such aesthetic judgements could not be demonstrated; but he claimed that they could be justified. The judgements of romantic criticism had to be distinguished from mere subjective opinions; they had to be given authority. 'We cannot prove our judgements', he wrote, 'but we can vindicate our right to make them.' The critic could vindicate his right to judge by acquiring a profound and extensive knowledge of the field – literature, art or music. In a word, the critic must be a scholar.

Friedrich Schlegel himself was a formidable scholar – deeply versed in the literature of several languages and the philosophies of several cultures. While rejecting classical aesthetics, he did not diminish, but rather enlarged his classical studies. 'Only the rereading of classical literature', he once said, 'can properly be called reading'. He believed that literary criticism should itself become a form of literature. The discovery and appraisal of the ideal inherent in a work of art could not be a process of mere description or analysis. In order to communicate what he called the 'necessary impression' of a poem, Schlegel insisted that the critic had to become a kind of poet as well as a scholar.

Herder's campaign to reawaken the public awareness of medieval arts and achievements found a new champion in Wilhelm Heinrich Wackenroder, who shared none of Schlegel's enthusiasm for classical antiquity. 'True art', he wrote 'is to be discovered rather among the pointed vaults and ornate edifices of medieval Germany than under Mediterranean skies.' He proceeded to claim for Albrecht Dürer, the German Renaissance painter, moral as well as aesthetic virtues, as the authentic recorder, in his portraits, of the pure souls and upright characters of earlier German people; and in a similar vein Wackenroder praised early church music for giving voice to those people's genuine religious feelings. He argued that the Gothic architecture of Nuremberg and the Franconian towns gave expression to a Christian morality which was superior to the pagan ethos proclaimed by the buildings of ancient Greece and Rome, suggesting that the better morals produced the better architecture.

Wackenroder drew attention to many Gothic masterpieces that eighteenth-century taste neglected, but which have since been generally recognized as among the finest creations of

European civilization. In the Saxon city of Naumburg for example, Wackenroder could point to the thirteenth-century cathedral, with its marvellous statues of the founders, Ekkehard and Uta, Gerburg, Hermann and Reglindis, not one of them a saint, but each a model of the human form idealized. In Bamberg he pointed to the figure of *Der Reiter*, to the *Dom*, to the bishop's palace, the *Rathaus* and the old Benedictine abbey, to prove that Germany contained art and architecture as worthy of attention as any in France or Italy and cities to stand comparison with Siena or Lucca or Chartres.

Some of the buildings that Wackenroder exalted as *Mittelalter* were classified by later historians as Renaissance, but Wackenroder was not a taxonomist; he was a poet, recreating the Middle Ages as myth, and as myth they entered the romantic imagination. In the manner of many Romantics, Wackenroder died poor and relatively unknown at the age of twenty-five. His best work was published after his death by his friend and fellow poet, Johann Ludwig Tieck, who lived to the age of eighty, wrote prolifically, asserted himself as a publicist of what Heine called *die romantische Schule*, and did much to make romanticism attractive to the *kleinbürgerlich*, or lower middle-class type of German reader as well as those in the higher ranks of society, to whom the romantic cult of medieval chivalry could be expected more readily to appeal.

Friedrich Schlegel, on the other hand, with his more Bohemian form of romanticism, chose to set himself at odds with the German bourgeoisie, at least in his younger years, though he became very conservative, conventional and pious with age. It must be said that he was less gifted as a creative writer than his brother, August Wilhelm, whose translations of Shakespeare's plays achieved such perfection that Shakespeare came to be read as a German dramatist, almost as German as Goethe himself. Friedrich Schlegel did, however, make at least one memorable contribution to creative literature – a novel in the style of *La nouvelle Héloïse* and *Werther*, but designed to press romanticism beyond the limits that Rousseau and Goethe had imposed upon themselves, a novel freer in structure and freer in its morality. *Lucinde* is in part an epistolary novel, in part an experimental one; between the letters sections of narration, dialogue and polemics appear in bewildering juxtaposition. Schlegel explained that his object in this design had been to combine 'the substance of a confession with the structure of an arabesque'. It is obvious, and was all too obvious to the readers of his time, that the central male character, Julius, is Schlegel himself. The novel describes Julius's love affair with a married woman, the Lucinde of the title. There is not much of a plot, but the message is unmistakable. Whereas both *La nouvelle Heloïse* and *Werther* record the triumph of conventional marriage over romantic love, in that Julie remains faithful to Wolmar and Lotte to Albert, Schlegel's novel records the triumph of romantic love over conventional marriage. It introduces a new, and significant figure into literature: the liberated woman. Schlegel's heroine Lucinde loves Julius, and she follows the promptings of her heart. She gives herself to Julius, and finds joy in his arms. True love is shown to be both spiritual and sensual. In order that no reader should overlook the sensual element, Schlegel describes their embraces in the sort of voluptuous detail which ensured for the book a *succès de scandale*. Moreover, Lucinde's adultery is shown to be unpunished: she finds happiness as well as love in the arms of Julius. Life between them 'flows like a beautiful song'.

Lucinde was all the more shocking to Schlegel's bourgeois contemporaries because it was generally known that the author was having an affair with Dorothea Veit, a Prussian banker's wife, and the book was seen as an unseemly exposure of their secrets. However, Schlegel claimed that the union of Lucinde and Julius was not really adulterous, but was more of a true marriage than the loveless bonds of conventional matrimony. Schlegel believed he was only carrying to its logical conclusion Rousseau's theory that love purifies sex. Besides, he balanced those parts in the work which certain critics said were like pages of French erotica with even more pages of philosophical thought.

The story has no ending, but one is suggested in a conversation between Julius and Lucinde: they exchange the thought that they might make their love eternal by dying together in the moment of its greatest intensity and bliss. There is both an echo here of the suicide of Werther and an intimation of the double suicide of Tristan and Isolde; but Schlegel preferred to leave his hero and heroine alive in the alcove.

Lucinde is a failure as a novel; its importance lies in the character of Lucinde and the ideal of the liberated woman she embodies, an ideal significantly different from that of the ideal woman of earlier romanticism, such as Julie or Lotte. For Lucinde is shown to be the equal of her lover in all things; their masculinity and femininity are said to be interchangeable; Lucinde is the friend, companion and soul-mate as well as the mistress of Julius. Whereas Rousseau had always insisted on the differences between male and female and proposed in *Émile* that a woman should be educated only for domesticity and modesty and the service of a man's moral needs, Schlegel's ideal woman was as emancipated and as cultured as a man. Not only in this novel but elsewhere, Schlegel pleaded for women to receive the same upbringing, the same education and above all the same freedom as men. His Lucinde was the first of a long line of liberated women in fiction and a no less impressive succession in real life – from George Sand and Mme de Staël to Colette and Vita Sackville-West. *Lucinde* was one of romanticism's few contributions to the literature of feminism.

The romanticism of the *Jenaer Kreis* was meant to be a way of life as much as an aesthetic doctrine, defying convention in all things. Not only did Dorothea Veit leave her husband to live with Schlegel, Sophie Bernhardi left her husband after an affair with Schlegel's elder brother, Wilhelm, who afterwards moved in with Caroline Böhmer, who, in turn, left Wilhelm for the philosopher Schelling. None of these couplings and uncouplings was undertaken in the spirit of insouciant hedonism which characterized upper-class life in the France of Louis XV; all were conducted with holy earnestness, following the example of Julius and Lucinde and in obedience to Schlegel's precept that 'the rights of love are higher than the ceremonies of the altar'.

Goethe was disgusted by *Lucinde* both aesthetically and morally. In his eyes a novel with no plot was a novel with no drama, and romantic drama could no more do without conflict than could classical; and if passion was not pitted against reason, passion must be pitted against passion. In the great work on which he was embarking, *Faust*, Goethe was to have love punished as cruelly as it is punished in any play by Racine. He believed wholeheartedly in the sanctity of conventional marriage, even though he hesitated for several years before marrying his own mistress. Neither Friedrich Schlegel nor any other member of the *Jenaer Kreis* was warmly welcomed at nearby Weimar, where Goethe had established himself as a pillar of society. Suspicion even extended in Goethe's household to younger poets whose romanticism was in no way as Bohemian or self-indulgent as Schlegel's.

Novalis, who had studied under Fichte as earnestly as Schlegel, was an unblemished champion of conventional rectitude and other-worldly idealism. Where Schlegel sought to achieve a synthesis of the spiritual and the sensual, with an embarrassing emphasis on the sensual, Novalis developed a conception of love that was essentially spiritual. This was all the more opportune in that the great love of his life, Sophie von Kühn, was a girl of thirteen when he became engaged to her, and fifteen when she died.

Novalis had received a pious Moravian upbringing, and the philosophical quest for the absolute, to which he was summoned by Fichte, became for him a genuinely religious quest. As he visualized his beloved Sophie in paradise, he identified her with the Virgin Mary, imagined her in the arms of Jesus and sometimes saw visions of her in heavenly robes as he knelt beside her grave. Fichte, he complained, had propounded a theory of imagination without having any imagination. Novalis himself let his imagination soar. He claimed that since imagination was the realm of poetry, it followed that the poet must know more than the philosopher who disciplined imagination by rules of logic and coherence.

He also suggested that because the poet lived in another world, he was bound to be a stranger in the everyday world. Sometimes Novalis suggested that the *Heimat*, or true home, of the poet was in a lost golden age, sometimes that it was in the future, sometimes in a distant present foreign land. In his unfinished novel *Heinrich von Ofterdingen*, the hero finds a book written in a language he does not know but which he is able mysteriously to understand; he reads in it the story of his own life, which is haunted by a 'blue flower'. From Novalis's notes for the novel it seems he intended to end it with Ofterdingen plucking the 'blue flower'. As for what the 'blue flower' symbolizes, Novalis gives us various intimations; the infinite, perhaps, or the *Heimat* or the eternal heavens beyond death. His 'blue flower' became an enduring symbol in German romanticism, at least until the student rebels of 1968 proposed 'to dye the blue flower red'.

Novalis himself was neither a political nor a social rebel. His aspirations were too spiritual. But he had a vision of a better order for the world, and it is one which had something in common with Herder's and Wackenroder's idealized picture of the Middle Ages; only his vision was of a European rather than a German past. In a posthumous essay entitled 'Christendom and Europe', Novalis envisages the recovery of the universal church that held the peoples of medieval Europe together in the bonds of common faith and worship, of fellowship and peace.

His imagination carried him not only towards the religious, but also towards the *magisch* or magical. In one of his fragments he wrote: 'the world must be romanticized; only then can we discern its original meaning'; he explained that by 'romanticizing' he meant 'giving a higher meaning to the ordinary and the appearance of infinity to the finite'. The poet who succeeds in doing this is a 'magician'.

Novalis was interested in the sciences, including the more controversial ones such as astrology, phrenology, alchemy and mesmerism, but by no means excluding the mainstream disciplines. He qualified himself for a professional career in mining, and even entertained the idea of editing a German encyclopaedia as comprehensive as Diderot's. He once said 'the universe is within us, but we must also look outwards to try to understand the world'. In his various activities, he worked extremely hard and without consideration for his health.

His *Hymns to Night*, first published in Schlegel's *Athenaeum* in 1800, are all too plainly hymns to death, expressing not simply that diffuse yearning for the infinite which is to be found in so much romantic poetry, but an unambiguous yearning for 'the sleep that is an eternal dream'. Night – or death – holds out to him the promise of the highest ecstasy – reunion with Sophie in the presence of Christ. After Novalis died of consumption at the age of twenty-nine, Tieck said that 'the visible and invisible worlds were one to him, and he distinguished life from death only by his longing for the latter'.

At Dresden Novalis had the opportunity of seeing the paintings of Caspar David Friedrich. In that most romantic of German artists there is something of the spirit of Novalis's poetry – not simply in the loving depiction of simple Christian scenes, but in the endeavour to 'give the finite the appearance of the infinite'. Natural scenery in Friedrich's paintings is somehow transformed into the supernatural, and the effect is all the more striking in those scenes where a dark figure is shown in silhouette in the foreground, with its back to the spectator, a Fichtean ego, sometimes dwarfed by, and sometimes commanding what it contemplates.

Friedrich, who came from the same sort of pious Protestant background as Novalis, sometimes spoke of nature as 'Christ's Bible', without, however, seeking as an artist to copy directly from nature. Although there are mountains and icebergs in his paintings, Friedrich never visited the Alps, let alone the Arctic. He saw with his 'mind's eye', as well as his eyes, aiming, as he once explained, to depict not things but rather 'God in things'. The most famous of his paintings, *Der Wanderer über dem Nebelmeer*, is probably to be understood as a self-portrait, and a confident one, for the figure we see with his back to us contemplating the peaks and summits through the mists, stands erect and firm on a rock; it is as if he has found, in communion with the invisible made visible, the peace that Novalis himself could only find in death.

The name of Hölderlin is commonly connected with that of Novalis, if only because they were near contemporaries and because they were the two best German poets of their generation; but Hölderlin had only a limited acquaintance with Novalis and no desire to be admitted to Schlegel's circle; he wished only to have the friendship of Schiller. Hölderlin thought of himself as a classical poet, and was not unjustified in doing so, but Schiller regarded him rather as a romantic Hellenist, and the friendship he bestowed on him was reserved and guarded although he did help find him employment as a private tutor. Hölderlin was at all events a romantic personality, another anti-hero defeated by life. Novalis, by contrast, was almost fortunate; he desired death and he died an early death. Hölderlin's career was a succession of failures and frustrations, ending with his descent into madness:

Woe is me, when from
A self-inflicted wound my heart is bleeding, and
Peace is utterly lost.

Hölderlin was of humble social origins and educated at con-
vent schools in Denkendorf and Maulbronn before attending
Tübingen University where classical studies were cultivated
with singular enthusiasm and theological students encouraged to see the presence of God in the visible world. This left
Hölderlin with a life-long passion for everything Greek and a
readiness to join Rousseau in the worship of nature. He was
not excited by the cult of the medieval, nor was he uncritical
of the fashionable Fichtean philosophy. He suggested that if
it was the destiny of nature to be overcome, as Fichte argued,
then the ego destroys the non-ego and in so doing removes
the very occasion of its ethical activity. Nature, for Hölderlin,
was not simply Fichte's 'external world', but the element in
which man moves and lives, a reality that is felt and experienced aesthetically.

As a student, Hölderlin believed no less than did Novalis
in the fusion of philosophy and poetry, and in time he too
lost confidence in philosophy and looked on poetry as the
voice of truth. 'Man is a god when he dreams; a beggar when
he reflects'. Only Hölderlin was less drawn to Christianity;
the mythical deities of the Greeks seemed to him to offer a
better insight into the meaning of life.

As a classical scholar he had hopes, which were disappointed, of a university appointment. Moreover, in his job as
a private tutor he fell in love, like Rousseau's St-Preux, with
his employer, a married woman named Susette Gontard, who
proved to be another Julie or Lotte, leading him on but
finally choosing to remain faithful to her husband. The end of
the affair with Susette marked what Hölderlin called the
'death' of his heart, an event all the more catastrophic for him
because his Hellenistic mythology defined his heart as the

vessel of divine presence, so that in allowing his heart to die he somehow felt he had betrayed his duty to the gods.

His poems became progressively more doom-laden. His earliest work is illuminated by the Rousseauesque view that nature is innocent and that all evil in the world is the work of society, but later Hölderlin came to believe that there is evil in nature itself and that man is born into corruption. In this acceptance of what is in effect a doctrine of original sin, Hölderlin adopts some of the idioms of Christianity, and indeed his last poems acquire a prophetic quality. But as he wrote of the deity as the 'God of Gods' and saw Christ's crucifixion as 'a tragedy', the Hellenistic element cannot be said to have been foresaken. In any case, the onset of madness diminished Hölderlin's capacity for coherent utterance even while he was still producing poems of extraordinary beauty.

Heinrich Heine, a somewhat hostile critic despite his own debt as a lyric poet to the German Romantics, suggested that they were prompted by a pantheistic impulse of which they were unaware and that their nostalgia for the medieval church, for folkloric culture, mysticism, magic and the rest of it was an 'unconscious attraction to the pantheism of the ancient Germans'. If this was far from true of Hölderlin, it was perhaps true of Novalis and even more true of Heinrich von Kleist, the most existentialist writer of his time. A man of noble birth, Kleist was pushed at an early age into the only career open to a Prussian aristocrat, that of an army officer. He 'wasted', as he put it, seven years of his life before he could break free to pursue the study of philosophy and cultivate his talents as a writer. Philosophy disappointed Kleist. He looked for metaphysical certainty, but his reading of Kant led him to the disturbing conclusion that there was no absolute truth and no absolute goodness. Like Nietzsche and Heidegger in later generations he was not persuaded by Kant's restoration of reason to its place in man's understanding of the universe after he had removed it from the universe itself;

he accepted only the destructive part of Kant's system and regarded the universe as meaningless. Deprived of the certainty he yearned for, Kleist was lost in the world, changeable and undecided in all he did. Reduced to belief that action alone could establish anything worthwhile, he found no satisfaction in any of the acts with which he experimented.

Although he was never a member of the *Jenaer Kreis*, Kleist gives more powerful expression to certain romantic themes than any contributor to the *Athenaeum*: the estrangement from bourgeois society, a pervasive sense of yearning or *Sehnsucht*, a restless anxiety, sadness and loneliness, and a fascination with darkness and death. Yet there is no moral anchorage in his work. In *Michael Kohlhaas*, for example, Kleist proclaims the sovereignty of private conscience over external authority; in *Die Hermannsschlacht* he proclaims the sovereignty of external authority over private conscience. His behaviour was equally incoherent: at one moment he tried to enlist in Napoleon's army, at another he called on all Germans to fight Napoleon. He became engaged to a general's daughter, and then went to extraordinary lengths to make her break the engagement. He was also unlucky: the Berlin theatre management refused to put on his plays and the Prussian government sabotaged the newspaper he launched to expound his views. Goethe befriended Kleist to the extent of staging his play *Der zerbrochene Krug* at Weimar, but the production was a failure, and Goethe kept the author at bay; he shrank from emotional young writers, perhaps seeing in them something he dreaded in himself. Goethe once said that Kleist troubled him 'like a man affected with an incurable disease'.

At the age of thirty Kleist found a 'cause' – nationalism. He is sometimes said to have become 'reactionary' after Napoleon's defeat of Prussia, but it is Friedrich Schlegel who can more properly be said to have turned reactionary – for he moved from his yearning for the medieval church to membership of the existing Catholic church and from dreams of liberty to service of the Austrian Empire as Metternich's publicist. Kleist remained the visionary as he called upon his countrymen to create something that did not yet exist, to realize the dream of a united Germany, a single *Vaterland*. Unhappily Kleist was not satisfied even with the service of this exalted cause. He itched for action, physical, violent action; action even as an end itself. When a woman friend told him she was terminally ill and wished to die, Kleist took her to the banks of the Wannsee, shot her, and then shot himself.

Kleist's vision of a new united Germany, however, had other adherents. A new school of romantic writers of Kleist's own age emerged in Heidelberg at the beginning of the nineteenth century, the *Jungere Romantik*, as they came to be called, inspired by a rather different concept of freedom from that of the *Jenaer Kreis* – national freedom as distinct from personal freedom. This group of writers, led by Clemens Brentano, Achim von Arnim and Joseph von Görres, were no less idealistic than the earlier Romantics, but theirs was a less inward romanticism, with a public as well as a private dimension, political as well as ethical. The philosopher they looked to was still Fichte, but Fichte himself had modified his teaching significantly in response to the events of the French Revolution and the Napoleonic Wars.

In 1789, Fichte the liberal individualist had welcomed the French Revolution with its promise to enthrone the rights of the individual; but by the turn of the century when the French threatened to conquer the whole of Europe, Fichte had turned into a German nationalist, ceased to talk about the rights of man and started instead to proclaim only the collective right of the German people to rule itself. Disenchantment with developments in France was not the only reason for this *volte-face*; Fichte was also influenced by further reflection on the political thought of Rousseau. For Rousseau himself, developing his theory of freedom between the *Dis-*

course on Inequality and such later writings as *The Social Contract*, had argued that the individualistic freedom which each man enjoyed in the state of nature could be improved upon if it were exchanged for a collective freedom which a group of men could enjoy together in the right sort of state, and this superior form of freedom Rousseau called civil freedom. Individual freedom was a gift of God which men lost when they submitted to the rule of despots – as they almost always had done in human history. Civil freedom they could achieve for themselves if only they could institute a form of political society in which they kept sovereignty in their own hands. The free individual was the man who ruled himself and correspondingly the free society was the society which ruled itself. This could only come about if the members of a society contracted together to transform themselves into a political society and institute a state that was united, autonomous and independent.

The lesson for Germany, as Fichte saw it, was clear. Herder had already depicted Germany as a cultural society: to achieve freedom, as Rousseau had defined it, the Germans would have to take the further deliberate step of establishing themselves as a political society. Tradition was the basis of the German cultural nation; will was now needed to create a German state. Having adopted Rousseau's theory of civil freedom as something which can only be experienced collectively, Fichte declared that no German could be free unless all Germans were free. Freedom must be national freedom; the rights of man were to be restated as the rights of the people. The new self which could, and should, be liberated was a national self.

This revised version of Fichtean philosophy is what captured the minds of the *Jungere Romantik* of Heidelberg. Brentano had started out as very much a Bohemian romantic on the Jena model, seeking self-realization in perpetually changing his studies from engineering to law, from medicine to philosophy, and then simply wandering round the countryside with a rucksack and guitar like a medieval *Spielmann*. He had made the acquaintance at Jena of the Schlegels and Tieck, and his first book – a novel, *Godwi*, which came out in 1800 – is obviously modelled on *Lucinde*, if notably less offensive to bourgeois sensibilities.

Brentano also possessed a natural gift, which went together with his love of music, for lyric poetry, a gift he cultivated when he married a woman poet, Sophie Schubart and, having settled with her in Heidelberg, became the friend and collaborator of Achim von Arnim, who, in turn, married Brentano's sister, Bettina, another poet who was to achieve literary fame in her own right. This was one significant difference between Jena and Heidelberg: whereas the women of the *Jenaer Kreis* served as inspirational companions to the poets, in the 'second generation' of German romanticism, women were poets themselves. Sophie Brentano had enjoyed the admiration of Schiller, and contributed to his *Musenalmanach*, and being several years older than her husband, had seen her *Gedichte* in print in the same year as his first novel. Bettina von Arnim's renown came rather later, but what is striking about her work is that it does not deal with the proverbial women's domestic themes, but with social and political subjects, and from a perspective more radical than that of most male poets among her contemporaries.

At Heidelberg Clemens Brentano and Achim von Arnim embarked on a project similar to that of Herder's *Volkslieder* of 1778, collecting together German songs and lyrics, which they published in three volumes called *Des Knaben Wunderhorn*, taking its title from the old folk tale about a boy who presents his queen with a magic horn. Their aim was even more sharply focused than that of Herder on the revival of a national spirit: their purpose unequivocally political where Herder's had been cultural.

Their success prompted another member of the Heidelberg group, Joseph von Görres, to edit a further collection of

German folk literature, *Die teutschen Volksbucher*, followed by yet another collection of old German folksongs *Altdeutsche Volks- und Meisterlieder*. A short-lived Heidelberg journal *Zeitung für Einsiedler* attracted writers from other parts of Germany, notably the brothers Jacob and Wilhelm Grimm, whose collections of German fairy tales or *Märchen* reached a vast public in many countries besides Germany. The Grimms were scholars whose purpose was to establish the fairy tale as something derived from German folklore as distinct from 'children's fiction' made up by modern authors. They went on, as philologists and lexicographers, to perform for the German language something analogous to the services undertaken for the French language by the Académie Française.

There were also among the Heidelberg group some poets who were purely poets, the most notable of whom was Joseph Freiherr von Eichendorff. His lyrical voice was unmatched by any of his contemporaries. A nobleman of ancient lineage, he fought, after his studies at Heidelberg, in the *Lutzowische Freikorps* against Napoleon. Although he lost his estates in Silesia as a result of the wars, he was the least politically *engagé* among the poets of his group. He was both a devout Catholic and a Rousseauesque worshipper of nature. His verses which are usually about love or nature, have all the qualities of song, and composers from Schumann and Mendelssohn to Richard Strauss set many of them to music. Eichendorff's finest poetry was the product of a quiet life as a civil servant, in which he also found time to write a few novels. The best known of these *Ahnung und Gegenwart* reveals how little faith he had in political as distinct from spiritual forces for the improvement of society.

Others, moving from Heidelberg to North Germany, became more active than ever in the nationalist cause. Görres edited the *Rheinische Merkur* for several years as a journal more political than literary. In Berlin Achim von Arnim and Clemens Brentano sought to give expression to their nationalist ideas in both prose and verse. On the occasion of the opening of the new University of Berlin, Brentano wrote a cantata *Universität Literarie* which makes it abundantly clear that his form of romanticism had adopted Fichte's concept of a higher positive form of freedom that can be experienced only in political society or, in other words, conferred by the state.

The cantata contains a stanza which reminds the students that they owe their freedom to the state:

> Der Staat, der euch ernährt,
> Der Staat, der von euch lernend, hoch euch ehret,
> Der Staat, der hohe Freiheit euch gewährt.
>
> *The state that nourishes you,*
> *The state that learns from you and esteems you highly,*
> *The state that guarantees your high freedom.*

It cannot escape notice that the state which is honoured in this poem is not the abstract German state exalted in other writings of the *Jungere Romantik*, but the concrete Prussian state which had established the University of Berlin. By no means all German Romantics were ready to accept this fusion of the ideal state with an actual state, and the implied assertion that Germany was Prussia magnified; but there had clearly emerged by 1810 in German romanticism a conservative tendency which matched that represented by Chateaubriand and Victor Hugo in French, and by Burke and Coleridge in English romanticism. The rich ambiguity of the concept of freedom had already begun to nourish ideologies of both left and right, and continued to do so almost everywhere.

But in at least one respect German romanticism remained unique. Whereas the Romantics of other countries distanced themselves from their universities and academies, German romanticism, with its heavy emphasis on the value of scholarship, its association with philosophy, and its national cultural mission, virtually took over the German universities. Many, perhaps most, of the scholars who made the German universities in the nineteenth century the best in the world were profoundly influenced by romanticism. The Romantics called the scholars from the study of texts to the study of contexts, to conduct research on the influence of religion, customs and laws on literature and the influence of literature on religion, customs and laws. Karl von Savigny adopted this programme in his celebrated history of Roman law in the Middle Ages, as did Friedrich von Raumer in his history of the Hohenstaufen and their times, and Barthold Niebuhr in his history of Rome. If the University of Jena was the first to bring together the philosophers and the poets, the University of Heidelberg was awakened from pedantic slumbers by the presence of the *Jungere Romantik*; Göttingen, an eighteenth-century foundation, was saved from becoming an upper-class finishing school by the romantic broadening of the study of law to include the study of literature; Friedrich Wilhelm von Schelling, a colleague and follower of Fichte at Jena, transported the romantic ethos to the universities of Würzburg and Munich, in the form he called transcendental idealism; the University of Berlin attracted from its inception the stars of romantic scholarship as its professors.

Their transformation of the German universities was assisted by circumstance. The Napoleonic Wars effectively put an end to the existence of twenty-two of the old German universities and those which survived were open to reconstruction. The romantic movement in Germany was thus not faced, as it was in France and England, with powerful academic institutions hostile or indifferent to its purposes. The institutions of German culture were vessels waiting to be filled, and exponents of romanticism filled them. Hence romanticism attained in Germany an importance which far exceeded its importance in any other country. It gave shape and substance to the culture of the new nation which emerged from the devastation of the Napoleonic wars.

3

English Romanticism

It is one of the ironies of history that the first philosopher of romanticism in England should have been one of the most savage critics of Rousseau, Edmund Burke. Burke's quarrel with Rousseau, however, was political, prompted by his belief that Rousseau's writings had inspired the French Revolution of 1789 which Burke considered a disaster. It was a much younger Edmund Burke who published in 1756 his *Philosophical Inquiry into the Origins of our Ideas on the Sublime and the Beautiful*, an attack on rationalism and classical formalism in art and an argument for what was afterwards known as romantic aesthetics.

An Irishman of modest origins who developed with the aid of a good deal of imagination and panache from a hack journalist into an English country gentleman and parliamentary orator, Burke's life was as romantic in its way as his philosophy. He was one of Diderot's 'originals', imposing himself on the world as a personality of his own invention. His critique of classicism begins with a refutation of the principle that clarity is an essential quality of great art. On the contrary, Burke argues, what is greatest and noblest in art is the infinite, and the infinite, having no bounds, cannot be clear and distinct. 'It is one thing to make an idea clear,' he writes, 'and another to make it affective to the imagination.' And it is the imagination, Burke insists, that all art must address: the imagination, not reason. Through imagination art must reach the passions. He claims that 'a great clearness', far from stirring the passions, 'is in some sense an enemy to all enthusiasm.'

Against the then fashionable view of the abbé du Bos that painting is an art superior to poetry because of the greater clarity that painting achieves in representation, Burke claims that poetry is superior to painting precisely because poetry can better render obscurity and ambiguity: 'It is our ignorance of things that causes all our admiration and chiefly excites our passions'. Eternity, Burke suggests, is among the most affecting ideas we have, and yet we understand very little about it. 'A clear idea', he goes so far as to say, 'is another name for a little idea.'

The main thrust of Burke's *Inquiry* is to revise prevailing conceptions of the sublime and the beautiful. He maintains that the sublime is that which arouses delight, while the beautiful is that which excites love. He goes on, more provocatively, to assert that feelings of fear are part of our delight, and even that we can witness with pleasure the distress of others. Delight, Burke says, is unconnected with reasoning or with utilitarian moral commands to diminish pain and enlarge the happiness of our fellow men. 'Whatever is fitted in any sort to excite the ideas of pain and danger is a source of the sublime.' Of all passions, fear most effectively robs the mind of its powers. And fear is an element of the astonishment which is provoked in our souls by the great and sublime in nature. It is also part of the awe which is generated by our consciousness of God; 'whatever, therefore, is terrible is sublime too'.

Burke connects this terror, in turn, with power, although he notes that useful power, the strength of a domesticated creature, such as an ox, has nothing of the sublime about it. It is untamed strength that is sublime as it 'comes upon us in the gloomy forest and in the howling wilderness in the form of the lion, the tiger, the panther or rhinoceros'. Burke also contrasts the impact on the imagination of the prospect of a flat stretch of landscape with the sight of an ocean: the ocean stirs the mind because it 'is the object of no small terror. Indeed terror is in all cases whatsoever . . . the ruling principle of the sublime'.

About beauty Burke has less to say. He dismisses those classical aesthetic doctrines which define beauty in terms of 'proportion', 'fitness' and 'moral perfection' on the grounds that such qualities appeal to the understanding or reason, whereas art speaks to the emotions. Having asserted that beauty is that which excites love, Burke leaves no doubt in the reader's mind than he regards love as a less important passion than those to which the sublime appeals, namely awe and all that is related to it. The greatest art reaches toward the sublime, and only the lesser art towards the beautiful.

The impact of Burke's aesthetics was not felt immediately in England, and was better appreciated elsewhere; his *Inquiry* was read by, among others, Diderot and Herder, who were more willing to acknowledge their debt to it than were Blake and Coleridge, for example, who attacked the philosopher while absorbing his philosophy. Blake and Coleridge began to make their names as poets at the beginning of the French Revolution, by which time Burke was better known for his politics than for his theory of art, and his politics were highly controversial.

Two conflicting responses to the French Revolution could equally be considered romantic. The first, almost instinctive, reaction was favourable, and this was the reaction of Blake, Coleridge, Wordsworth, Southey and perhaps most English poets of their generation, as of Fichte, and many young Romantics in Germany. These writers saw the Revolution as a rising of the people of France in support of freedom –

freedom being one of the most sublime ideals to which the human heart could aspire. Burke regarded the French Revolution differently. He did not see it as a struggle for freedom, but as a wholly rationalist endeavour, aimed at altering the society and institutions of France according to the abstract ideological designs of the Enlightenment. Thus Burke's response to the Revolution was to condemn it. In his *Reflections on the Revolution in France* he justified his attitude with a systematic exposition of a romantic form of conservatism which was anathema to radicals in 1790, but which was to find favour after further reflection by many who at first rejected it, if only because the French Revolution developed with the passage of time aspects less attractive to the liberal mind.

Burke's romantic conservatism rested, like the romantic nationalism of Herder in Germany, on a belief in the primacy of history − as opposed to the empiricist sociology of the Enlightenment − for its understanding of society and the human condition. In his *Reflections*, Burke argued that the kingdom of France was, like any other nation, the product of historical experience and of growth analogous to that of a living organism. While he did not categorically reject the fashionable liberal view that society was contractual in its origins, Burke insisted that the 'social contract' on which any civil society was based is 'not a partnership in things of a temporary and perishable nature. It is a partnership in all art; a partnership in every virtue and in all perfection . . . a partnership between those who are living, those who are dead and those who are yet to be born.' He protested that a society whose members had lived together through so many generations, united under a common sovereign by habit, custom and tradition ought not to be torn apart, as the Revolutionaries were tearing France apart, with the aim of making everything afresh. Burke was accused by his critics of glamorizing the Bourbon royal family, and especially the Queen, together with the clergy and nobility in his picture of the French *ancien régime*, but it was an important part of his philosophy to cherish the myths and magic of ancient institutions together with the deep-seated preferences and prejudices which united people in a civil harmony. He was wholly in favour of correcting perceptible abuses and reforming defective laws, but revolution of the sort that the French had started – the total reordering and rebuilding of society – he considered almost sacrilegious.

Had Burke possessed a greater knowledge than he did of Rousseau's thinking, he might have found in it much that was in accord with his own ideas, but Burke's Rousseau was simply the author of *The Social Contract*, Rousseau transformed into an ideologue of populist tyranny by Robespierre and St-Just; and so in his *Reflections* Burke castigated the very philosopher he might have acknowledged as an intellectual ancestor. Burke in turn was castigated by writers who owed much to the ideas that he had originated. Among these was William Blake the author of *Songs of Innocence and Experience*.

William Blake detested Burke, but he often said in verse things that Burke had said in prose in the *Inquiry*, a book that had been published a year before Blake was born. Burke's remark about the sublime coming upon us 'in the gloomy forest' in the form of the lion, the tiger and other such wild beasts is echoed in Blake's most famous poem:

> Tyger! Tyger! burning bright
> In the forests of the night,
> What immortal hand or eye
> Could frame thy fearful symmetry?

Like Burke, Blake believed in the supremacy of the sublime over the beautiful; he, too, maintained that the highest aim of art was to express the inexpressible; that poetry must necessarily be obscure, that fear was part of our apprehension of the divine, and that 'the world of Imagination is the world of Eternity'. He was a master at once of compressed, symbolic utterance and of lyrical, musical language:

> To see a World in a Grain of Sand
> And a Heaven in a Wild Flower
> Hold Infinity in the palm of your hand
> And Eternity in an hour.

Blake was an untutored genius, a poor shopkeeper's son, whose only schooling was what he received as an engraver's apprentice and as an art student at the Royal Academy. His first quarrel with the classical tradition was with the leading teacher at the Academy, Sir Joshua Reynolds, whose principles of art he rejected scornfully. Blake went on to develop his own talents as a draughtsman and painter with the encouragement of the Swiss immigrant Fuseli, whose paintings are rich in fantasy. Blake's paintings, however, were visionary rather than fantastical, closer in a way to Caspar David Friedrich's, in that they attempt to depict the unseen in the seen, the supernatural in the natural. It could even be said that such was what Blake actually saw with his singular powers of perception. A self-taught reader of philosophy as well as of literature, Blake attacked the prevailing empiricist view that all knowledge reaches the mind through the senses: the imagination, he insisted, was the faculty which gave access to truth. 'Mental Things are alone Real', he wrote, 'what is call'd Corporeal Nobody knows of its Dwelling place; it is Fallacy and its Existence an Imposture.' Blake's homespun philosophy was groping towards what was to become in the thought of more sophisticated contemporaries, such as Coleridge, idealism.

Blake's temperament, however, was more religious than philosophical:

> I am in God's presence night and day
> And He never turns His face away.

Part of Blake's strength as a poet was his absolute honesty. There is in his work none of the poses and empty formalities and polite hypocrisies which are so easily acquired with a classical education; he has an extraordinary insight into human emotions, and a simple way of saying what he knows. 'This makes him,' as T. S. Eliot once put it, 'terrifying'.

Blake's *Songs of Innocence* came out in 1789, the first year of the French Revolution, and was followed five years later by his *Songs of Experience*. Although they were not properly appreciated at the time, these books marked a turning point in English poetry, the beginning of a romantic epoch in which other names were soon to be added to Blake's – among others Wordsworth, Coleridge, Southey, Shelley, Keats and Byron. Blake's two sets of songs illustrate a theme which was central to Rousseau's thinking: the contrast between the goodness of nature and the corruption of civilization. In the *Songs of Innocence* we hear the voice of childhood, recalling the pleasures of the life of nature, in *Songs of Experience* that of the grown man, socialized man, *l'homme civil* as Rousseau called him, trapped in the prisons of state and church. In childhood, all is spontaneous and true; in maturity, all is corruption, hypocrisy, jealousy, vanity, cruelty and envy; the natural play of affection is poisoned:

> O Rose, thou art sick!
> The invisible worm,
> That flies in the night
> In the howling storm,
>
> Has found out thy bed
> Of crimson joy;
> And his dark secret love
> Does thy life destroy.

Such is the richness of his symbolism that Blake is able to say in two quatrains what Rousseau says in many pages of philosophical argument. Blake had perhaps rather less faith than Rousseau in the goodness of natural man, but he had correspondingly greater belief in Christ as the saviour of us all. Because of Christ's redemption, a good society, Blake believed, was within man's grasp and he called upon his contemporaries to create such a better world: 'Rouze up, O Young Men of the New Age', he cried when the French Revolution broke out; for if Burke was a Romantic of the Right, Blake was very much a Romantic of the Left. Prompted by the events of 1789 in France, he envisaged the creation of what he called 'Jerusalem' in England. This meant the casting off of conventional ideas, not only in politics, but in society and the family as well, the abolition of hierarchies in church and state, the liberation of women no less than of men and the inauguration of the rule of love. The basis of such a revolution, Blake insisted, must be changes in the inner being of individuals even more than in the structure of the state. 'Religion and Humility' were the moral forces he named and on which he pinned his hopes.

The one revolution Blake opposed was the industrial revolution; the 'dark Satanic mills' he indicted in a celebrated line represented all the industrial installations, factories, mines, technologies and scientific innovations which were taking men away from the land and the artisans' workshops to become slaves of machines in ugly dirty cities. It has been argued by Marxist historians that the triumph of romanticism and the cult of nature in England from the later eighteenth century onwards is to be understood as a reaction against industrialization – a fastidious upper-class reaction – but if it was such, it was the plebeian William Blake who gave the earliest and most eloquent expression to it.

A poet who shared the ideas and aspirations of Blake as a young man and those of Burke in middle age was Samuel Taylor Coleridge. Blake wrote 'I must Create a System, or be enslaved by another Man's', but he did not have the intellectual culture to create a philosophical system. Coleridge did.

The son of a clergyman–scholar, well educated at Christ's Hospital and Cambridge, he achieved eminence as much as a philosopher as a poet. John Stuart Mill praised his 'seminal mind' and his 'unique contribution to the philosophy of human culture'. Indeed, after studying both German philosophy and the literary criticism of *die romantische Schule* in Germany, Coleridge became in effect the leading theorist of romanticism in nineteenth-century England.

In 1789 Coleridge welcomed the French Revolution as eagerly as did Blake. And like Blake he yearned to see great changes in England, the creation of a New Jerusalem based not only on modifications of political structures, but on the emergence of a new kind of social man. Coleridge was only seventeen in 1789 and his enthusiasm for the French Revolution lasted less than four years. The turning-point was the invasion of Switzerland by the French revolutionary armies, an event which prompted Coleridge to express his disapproval and disillusionment in verse in 'France, an Ode':

> With what deep worship I have still adored
> The spirit of divinest liberty.

Coleridge protested that he had not lost his faith in the ideals which the French had once proclaimed, and then violated; he only wished to find new ways of achieving them. The method he first favoured was that of establishing a small-scale harmonious community which could serve as a model for a more widespread social regeneration. He hoped to persuade a group of kindred spirits to join him in setting up such a utopia in miniature, sharing their property, working the land, and ruling themselves in egalitarian freedom; 'pantisocracy' was his name for this system.

In planning his community, Coleridge recruited the support of a fellow poet two years younger than himself, an undergraduate at Oxford named Robert Southey. Having been expelled from his school for attacking corporal punishment in a magazine article, Southey had become the archetypal student rebel. He proclaimed his sympathy for the French Revolution in a verse drama *Joan of Arc* and published a number of lyrical poems in minor literary journals. He liked Coleridge's idea of a pantisocracy, but insisted that it would have to be established in the New World. When the two young poets heard of a possible place beside the Susquehanna River in Pennsylvania, they invited twenty young friends to join them there. 'O'er the ocean swell,' Coleridge declared in verse 'Sublime of hope, I seek the cottag'd dell.'

The twenty young friends were chosen because they formed ten couples. Southey already had a wife and Coleridge allowed himself to be hurried into a marriage to Southey's wife's sister, so that the party could emigrate as twelve couples. It proved from the start an unhappy marriage, and it was not long before the whole pantisocratic scheme was abandoned. Southey shocked Coleridge by declaring that he would only go to Pennsylvania if he could take four servants with him and if he could keep all his private property, except for the shared ownership of the land. The quarrel lasted some time, but the poets' lives remained intertwined, if only because their wives were sisters and because they lived near each other in the West of England.

It was in the West of England that Coleridge made the acquaintance of William Wordsworth, who proved to be a better friend than Southey, and a better poet, even if Southey, four years his junior, was appointed Poet Laureate in preference to Wordsworth. The three poets formed a little literary circle, and when they moved North to houses near each other in the Lake District, in Westmorland, they entered history as the 'Lake Poets' or 'Lakists' as Sainte-Beuve called them.

Wordsworth, who made his name as a poet with 'An Evening Walk' in 1793, was a Cambridge man with much the same sort of middle-class Anglican background as Coleridge.

He had greeted the French Revolution with equal enthusiasm:

> Bliss was it in that dawn to be alive,
> But to be young was very heaven!

While Coleridge was lecturing about the French Revolution
in provincial English dissenters' meeting places, Wordsworth
went to France to witness the unfolding of the Revolution at
first hand. He made friends with republican activists and
acquired a French mistress, one Annette Vallon, who bore
him a child and with whom he was undoubtedly in love. Yet
for all his romantic philosophy, Wordsworth proved as un-
willing to marry the girl he loved as Coleridge was willing to
marry the girl he did not love. Once his illusions about
France and the Revolution were dispelled, Wordsworth returned to England to settle down in rural domesticity with
his sister Dorothy. 'Poetry', he once suggested, 'takes its
origins from emotions recollected in tranquillity'. Tranquillity was what he sought – successfully – for the rest of his life,
and he lived to be eighty.

In 1798 there appeared a volume of *Lyrical Ballads*, a joint
production of Wordsworth and Coleridge, which probably
did more than any other single work to redirect English taste
from the neo-classical to the romantic. Blake's *Songs of Innocence* and *Songs of Experience* had come out four years earlier,
but had passed almost unnoticed at the time. The *Lyrical
Ballads* were widely read, and established the two poets at the
head of their profession. Wordsworth once said that 'every
great and original writer must himself create the taste by
which he is to be relished'. With his prose essays and notably
in his Preface to the *Lyrical Ballads*, Wordsworth tried to do
just this. At that early stage of his collaboration with Coleridge, he assumed the leadership of the tandem. Only four
poems in the *Lyrical Ballads* were by Coleridge, although one
of them was 'The Rime of the Ancient Mariner', the most

remarkable contribution. Already there were significant differences between Wordsworth's idea of romantic poetry and Coleridge's. Wordsworth was an aesthete, Coleridge a metaphysician; Wordsworth was inspired by nature; Coleridge by the unseen world. Both subscribed to the central romantic doctrine of the supremacy of imagination, but each had his own conception of what that meant. Wordsworth was close to Rousseau in his love of the visible world as God had created it, and in his dislike of industrial arts and empirical sciences:

> Sweet is the lore which nature brings;
> Our meddling intellect
> Misshapes the beauteous forms of things:—
> We murder to dissect.
>
> Enough of science and of art;
> Close up those barren leaves;
> Come forth, and bring with you a heart
> That watches and receives.

Coleridge wanted more than a heart that watches and receives. He believed in mind and the necessity of thought. He valued scientific thinking as a branch of philosophy, subordinate to metaphysics. Indeed his highest praise of poetry was to assert that it is 'the most philosophic of all writing'. He said of poetry that 'its object is truth carried alive into the heart by passion'. If Coleridge's contribution to the *Lyrical Ballads* are as lyrical as Wordsworth's, his themes are far deeper, more sombre and arcane.

> My eyes make pictures when they are shut.

This dream quality of the scenery in Coleridge's poems makes it more, rather than less, vivid than the sunlit landscapes of Wordsworth's. Where memory furnishes the images for Wordsworth pure imagination is the faculty which Coleridge employs, and the element that Burke called 'terror' is seldom wholly absent; it is indeed what gives 'The Rime of the Ancient Mariner' its haunting power:

> Alone, alone, all, all alone,
> Alone on a wide wide sea!
> And never a saint took pity on
> My soul in agony.

Soon after the publication of the *Lyrical Ballads* Coleridge persuaded Wordsworth with his sister Dorothy to accompany him on a visit to Germany. Coleridge's purpose was to study the new German philosophy and the poetry of the German Romantics at the source, and he made his way at once to the University of Göttingen although that was not a centre of great literary activity. Wordsworth lingered in another German city. He was not attracted by the great professors. Already fluent in French, he felt no impulse to join Coleridge in studying the German language, let alone the German metaphysics. The sojourn in Germany meant little to Wordsworth, but it contributed much to the formation of Coleridge, both as a poet and as a philosopher, although he soon ceased to acknowledge any real distinction between the two: 'No man was ever yet a great poet, without being at the same time a profound philosopher.'

Friendship between Coleridge and Wordsworth was not diminished by their conflicting responses to the German experience. In Wordsworth's household in the Lake District, once Wordsworth had acquired a wife to join him there with his sister Dorothy, and that wife in turn brought in her sister Sara, Coleridge found a second home; the three women fussed over him agreeably and provided a welcome refuge from the company of his own nagging spouse. Wordsworth in the meantime became increasingly Rousseauesque, whether tramping the hills and valleys of the Lake District to commune with nature or working on his memory to produce his autobiographical *magnum opus, The Prelude*, an equivalent in verse of

Rousseau's prose *Confessions*, and the most sustained exploration of the self in English romantic literature.

Coleridge was far from healthy. Ever more afflicted with gout and addicted to opium, he sought his satisfactions in the realm of pure thought. He fell in love with Wordsworth's sister-in-law, but Anglican taboos were too strong among the Lake poets to permit him even to avow adulterous desires. He worked hard, always seeking to express his ideas systematically. He was not content to throw off lines like Wordsworth's 'Imagination is Reason in her most exalted mood'; he set out to analyse and clarify the concept of imagination in detail. He concluded that there are two sorts of imagination, both of which must be distinguished from 'fancy'. First there is primary imagination, something possessed by all men, and in the exercise of which human beings, who are made in God's image, repeat in perception God's creative act. Next there is secondary or poetic imagination, possessed only by artists, and the possession of which distinguishes the artist from ordinary men. This is the faculty by which the artist imposes order on the chaos of the universe and unifies the diverse elements of experience into significant form. By using poetic imagination, the artist, as Coleridge puts it, 'dissolves, diffuses, dissipates in order to create'. Fancy is of another order altogether. It is not creative, but aggregative; it is a universal human faculty, which stands together with memory and sense in the epistemology of the seventeenth-century philosopher John Locke. Coleridge's distinction between poetic imagination and fancy corresponds to the distinction drawn by some German philosophers of romanticism between genius and talent; talent works with fancy, genius with imagination.

It follows from this analysis that the faculties of observation and memory, which Wordsworth invoked as the sources of artistic activity, are not enough for Coleridge. He also demands constructive thought. The poet, writes Coleridge, 'must distance himself from nature in order to return to her with full effect'. Coleridge himself was not an especially close observer of nature in the first place. He once confessed in a letter: 'From whatever place I write you will expect that part of my "Travels" will consist of excursions in my own mind.' His eyes were focused inward.

By the turn of the century Coleridge was, in any case, too much of an invalid to enjoy travelling. He had also become a conservative. He had put away what he called his 'squeaking baby trumpet of sedition', and moved to the Right in company with Wordsworth, who returned to the traditional Anglican beliefs of his childhood, and of Southey, who became a regular contributor of political articles to the Tory *Quarterly Review*. Coleridge's conservatism, however, was of a rather more original kind than that of his fellow Lake poets; original enough to earn him a place as a political theorist, somewhere between Burke and Hegel. In writings such as *The Constitution of State and Church* Coleridge put the case for a political order in which a constitutional monarchy sustains a dialectical equilibrium between the traditionalist weight of the aristocratic interest and the progressive drive of bourgeois commercialism. This was not simply an idealized picture of England as it was, because Coleridge envisaged the development of a new kind of church, or 'clerisy' as he called it – a class of superior-minded men dedicated to the education of the populace and the enlargement of its culture. 'Cultivation' was his aim, and he distinguished it from 'civilization', or the material complex of advanced institutions, industries and so forth produced by progress in science and technology. He described cultivation as 'the harmonious development of those qualities and faculties that characterize our humanity', and it was on this process that he pinned his hopes. Coleridge in his mature, conservative years remained as much the 'idealist' as he had been in his radical youth, only culture had taken the place of liberty as the central focus of his aspirations, much as it had among certain Romantics of Germany.

As Coleridge and his contemporaries advanced into middle age, a new generation of English poets emerged to challenge their pre-eminence, and to reassert the radical, youthful, unconventional image of romanticism. Percy Bysshe Shelley, a beautiful youth, aristocratic, bold and scornful of authority, was expelled from his college at Oxford in March, 1811, at the age of eighteen for publishing an essay entitled 'The Necessity of Atheism'. In an England where Napoleon's threat had made the general public no less reactionary than the poets of the Lake District, Shelley could not expect much tolerance, but at least he enjoyed the attention that comes with notoriety, and he breathed new life into English poetry.

He subscribed to most of Coleridge's ideas about the nature of poetry, including the belief that the poet should be a philosopher. At one time or another, Shelley spoke of poetry as 'lifting the veil from the hidden beauty of the world' and 'making familiar things be as if they were not familiar', of poets as teachers of ideal truth, creators of new knowledge, and – in a much quoted phrase – of poets as 'the unacknowledged legislators of the world'. He also declared in the face of the flood tide of philistine reaction in the England of his time that 'poetry is rising from a new birth'.

Shelley was, and remained, a romantic of the Left. In pleading for the supremacy of the imagination, he suggested that part of its virtue lay in the fact that imagination enabled a man to sympathize with the sufferings of others. He did not sentimentalize the working man but protested against the exploitation of the poor by the rich:

> Men of England, wherefore plough
> For the lords who lay ye low?

Although he was the grandson of a baronet and was an Etonian who never had to earn his own living, Shelley expressed bitter indignation at the injustice of the social order in England and the futility of Christian charity as a remedy.

He did not possess what Coleridge thought of as the truly reflective disposition that a poet needed, but was rather a creature of the emotions, and as such he was closer to what the general public thought a romantic poet should be.

A few weeks after his expulsion from Oxford, Shelley met a girl named Harriet Westbrook who, though only sixteen years old, professed opinions as radical as his own, and he promptly took her to Scotland and married her. On their return they visited Coleridge and Wordsworth in the Lake District only to be shocked by their Tory political views, and had to look elsewhere for a more congenial guru. They found one in the person of William Godwin, who paradoxically combined adherence to the progressive empiricism of the Enlightenment with utopian visions of human brotherhood, and who encouraged Shelley to proclaim the sovereignty at once of reason and of love. Shelley's first important poem 'Queen Mab' is informed by this aspiration. Reason, the poem suggests, will triumph in its conflict with prejudice, establish the reign of freedom and prosperity, abolish hunger and want, and diminish the pain of death. Meanwhile, in the later *Prometheus Unbound*, Shelley envisages a morality soundly based on love – eternal love:

> Fate, Time, Occasion, Chance and Change? To these
> All things are subject but eternal love.

Love, however, proved less than eternal in Shelley's own heart. In 1814, soon after his wife Harriet had given birth to their first child, Ianthe, his eyes fell on another girl of sixteen, Godwin's daughter, Mary; and he promptly carried her off to Switzerland to visit sights made famous in the writings of Jean-Jacques Rousseau. Harriet was already pregnant with a second child by Shelley, and in November of that year she gave birth to a son, Charles. Shelley then returned to England, not to rejoin Harriet and his children, but to collect an inheritance of £1,000 a year, and he was soon back on the

shores of Lake Geneva with Mary. Harriet thereupon committed suicide, so that Shelley was free to marry Mary, who
had already given birth to his son, William, and who had also
taken up writing. Indeed, Mary soon established herself as an
author in her own right with her novel *Frankenstein*, published
in the same year as the birth of her second child by Shelley,
Clara.

Frankenstein has endured, a classic of science fiction, and
also a landmark in English literature, signalling the transi-
tion from the eighteenth-century Gothic tale, with all its
mysteries and ghosts and artificial horrors, to the deeply
serious romantic novel of the nineteenth century. Shelley
himself had yet to produce his own best work. This he did in
the four years spent with Mary in Italy between 1818 and
1822, immensely productive years, if also tragic ones, marked
by the deaths first of the baby Clara, then of William, and
finally of Shelley himself, drowned near Lerici at the age of
thirty.

The outstanding work of these four years is *Prometheus
Unbound*. This is a philosophical poem on the grand scale, and
the philosophy that informs it is no longer the progressive
optimism of William Godwin and *Queen Mab*, but something
derived from Shelley's reading of Plato and Aeschylus; its
theme is nothing less than the struggle between good and
evil in the history of mankind. Shelley's starting point was
the play of Aeschylus *Prometheus Bound*, in which Prometheus,
the friend of mankind, confronts Zeus, the tyrant of the
universe. Although Aeschylus never completed his projected
sequel to the play, he seems to have envisaged a reconciliation
of the two powers. Shelley could not accept the idea of such a
reconciliation between 'the champion and the oppressor of
mankind', so he decided to write a play with another outcome.
Shelley's Prometheus is a symbol of humanity idealized, of
man as 'the highest perfection of moral and intellectual
nature'. The Zeus of Aeschylus becomes Jupiter in Shelley's

play, and is depicted as embodying all the destructive forces of evil. Shelley stays close to the Greek myth in having the presiding god overthrown by his own son, to whom the poet gives the name of Demogorgon. This character symbolizes the spirit of life and energy, in which the natural forces of earth and sea are allied to those of human volition and vitality. Prometheus is supported in his travail by three companions who represent faith, hope and love, and as the play unfolds, Jupiter's destructive tyranny is matched when the powers of life and love are united. But there is no final victory: an endless conflict of good against evil is shown to be part of the destiny of man.

If Shelley had abandoned the atheism of his student years, it was not to acknowledge the existence of God as a benevolent· omnipotent father of his creatures; he sees God rather as a cruel despot against whom the human race has to assert and defend its goodness. Shelley's creed was, so to speak, Christianity inverted, suggesting both that God exists and that God is *not* love.

If news of Shelley's death was greeted with sorrow by every reader who had come to appreciate his poetry, it was also undoubtedly received with a certain public satisfaction. In creating a taste for romantic verse, the poets also created a taste for romantic lives. The examples of Werther, Kleist and Novalis had established the thought in people's minds that the complete romantic poet should die young, so that Shelley's readers might well have been disappointed if he had lived longer, and the dashing golden youth turned grey and prudent like the ageing poets of the Lakes. He had himself declared in 'The Daemon of the World':

> How wonderful is Death
> Death and his brother Sleep!

Shelley's friend John Keats wrote an ode to Thomas Chatterton, the mid-eighteenth-century youth who produced poems in the Gothic style of Ossian and then died by his own hand, impoverished and neglected in a squalid garret at the age of seventeen:

O Chatterton! How very sad thy fate!

No less sad was the fate of Keats himself, dying in 1821 at the age of twenty-five. He was one of the purest poets in the English language, and by all accounts the most lovable of men. He devoted months of his short life to nursing first his mother, then his brother while they were dying from consumption, and becoming infected himself in the process. His sweetness of nature earned him staunch friends, but his work was savaged by the critics. Not content with attacking his poems, these critics abused him as a person, treating him as a cockney upstart who had no business even to attempt to be a poet: all this because Keats came from a fairly humble background and had broken off his studies in surgery after taking only his apothecary's licence. 'Better be a starved apothecary than a starved poet', wrote one critic, 'Back to the shop, John.'

Keats's verses were romantic in a way which recalls the early work of Wordsworth, prompted like his by an emotional response to nature. However, when Keats met Wordsworth, he was disappointed to find him egoistic and pompous. Keats shrank from the cult of the self which Wordsworth had picked up from Rousseau and which, while inspiring an autobiographical masterpiece in 'The Prelude', also produced a charmless narcissism in the poet. Coleridge, also, had no particular personal attraction for Keats, nor had the Coleridgean project of fusing poetry with philosophy. Keats wrote:

In the dull catalogue of common things.
Philosophy will clip an Angel's wings.

But to Shelley, his contemporary, he was drawn by instinctive sympathy, even though he had no interest in the ideological speculations of men like Godwin who were Shelley's friends and mentors:

> The poet and the dreamer are distinct,
> Diverse, sheer opposite, antipodes.
> The one pours out a balm upon the world,
> The other vexes it.

As a very young man Keats declared that he wanted only 'sensations, not thoughts', but later he revised this attitude and described the purpose of poetry as being 'to soothe the cares and lift the thoughts of men'. He never ceased to plead for openness in thinking and for toleration: 'Let the mind be a thoroughfare for all thoughts. Not a select party.'

Keats was a modest poet, unimpressed by Burke's plea for the sublime in preference to the beautiful. For Keats:

> 'Beauty is truth, truth beauty,' – that is all
> Ye know on earth, and all ye need to know.

In a letter to a friend Keats declared 'I am certain of nothing but the holiness of the heart's affection and the truth of imagination – what imagination seizes as beauty must be truth.' The chief object of Keats's own 'heart's affection' was a girl named Fanny Brawne, but he was too poor and too overwhelmed with anxiety about his afflicted family to propose marriage to her until he was himself too ill to offer her any prospect of a future. Some friends thought he lacked the will to live, and at times he came near to confirming their judgement:

> Darkling I listen; and, for many a time
> I have been half in love with easeful Death . . .

This was clearly not in Keats's case a mere poetic fancy. And although his earliest inspiration as a poet was derived from nature, he became increasingly conscious of the unseen world and of the beauty of what he called 'ethereal things'. When

Keats spoke of the 'truth of the imagination' he was thinking of that faculty's power to go beyond appearance to seize reality itself. Several of his best poems were written in a few weeks of feverish activity in the spring of 1819 – the year before he died. In these verses his spirit soars beyond the perceptions of the senses:

> Heard melodies are sweet, but those unheard
> Are sweeter . . .

His response to 'ethereal things' was aesthetic, not as was that of Coleridge, for example, intellectual. Even so, Keats warmed to Coleridge more than he did to Wordsworth, and one of his last and finest works, the 'Ode on a Grecian Urn' comes close to being a philosophical poem, in that it depicts the urn as a symbol of the wisdom of the ages:

> Thou still unravish'd bride of quietness,
> Thou foster-child of silence and slow time . . .

Towards the end of the Ode, however, Keats addresses the urn with these lines:

> Thou, silent form, dost tease us out of thought
> As doth eternity . . .

In a paradoxical way the 'Ode on a Grecian Urn' is a philosophical poem against philosophy.

While Keats's closest friend among the poets of his time was Shelley, his name is commonly linked also with that of Byron, if only because the three poets were contemporaries, became famous at much the same time, died young and are all linked to- gether in the history books as Romantics. Byron, however, was romantic in a different sense from either Keats or Shelley. In the first place he did not subscribe with them to the central romantic doctrine of the sovereignty of imagination. Keats himself pointed this out in a letter to his brother:

> You speak of Lord Byron and me – There is this great
> difference between us. He describes what he sees. I
> describe what I imagine.

Byron himself spoke only scornfully of the faculty that
romanticism held sacred:

> It is the fashion of the day to lay great stress upon
> what they call 'imagination' and 'invention' . . . an Irish
> peasant with a little whiskey in his head will imagine
> and invent more than would furnish forth a modern
> poem.

As for the patriarchs of English romantic poetry, Byron wrote:

> Let simple Wordsworth chime his childish verse
> And brother Coleridge lull the babe at nurse.

The one living English poet that Byron admired was Shelley,
on whom he lavished his somewhat ill-starred friendship. As
for Keats, Byron lamented in verse his early death, which he
attributed to the hostility of the literary critics, while at the
same time maliciously expressing surprise that a poet 'without Greek' should have chosen to write verses on a Grecian
subject. Byron wrote only on subjects he knew about, one of
which was himself. This introspection helps to give his poetry
its romantic quality, although much of it seems hardly
romantic at all. Byron wrote in the style of Dryden and Pope;
he conformed to all the neo-classical rules of the early eighteenth century, and often it is wit more than imagination,
which confers distinction on his verse. Assuredly Byron wrote
about ideal love, but only to contrast it with love that was
actually known in human experience.

> In her first passion a woman loves her lover,
> In all the others all she loves is love.

Byron's voice is one of irony and mockery:

> Think you, if Laura had been Petrarch's wife,
> He would have written sonnets all his life?

If much of Byron's verse is other than romantic, there is no questioning his romantic *persona*; no other figure in the nineteenth century so completely embodied the popular image of the romantic poet or achieved such universal fame in the role. Byron was handsome in a dark and brooding way, he was rich, extravagant, outrageous and the lover of many women; he was lame, a lord and a fighter who died at the age of thirty-six in a war for the liberation of Greece. Goethe called him 'the greatest genius of the century'. Of course, he was not, but people who did not read English were ready to believe that such a thrilling person must be a divine poet and Byron's renown abroad was even greater than it was at home.

It was not all myth. Byron was totally dedicated to one romantic ideal in which many other poets of the romantic school in both England and Germany had lost faith, if only as a result of developments in revolutionary France, namely liberty. Byron was only one year old when the French Revolution began, but his passion for liberty was very close to that of those French noblemen who gave the Revolution its first impetus: Lafayette, Condorcet, Mirabeau. His understanding of liberty was also theirs: liberty meant nothing less than, and nothing more than the abolition of tyranny.

> For I will teach, if possible, the stones
> To rise against earth's tyrants.

Byron had no interest in more rarified or republican notions of freedom which were inspired by thinkers such as Rousseau – 'the self-tormenting sophist'. Still less was he impressed by the metaphysical or moral concepts of freedom proclaimed by the German idealists and Coleridge. And yet, despite his being such an aristocratic liberal and having inherited a fortune as well as the peerage at the age of ten, Byron had very little sympathy with the English landowning classes:

For what were all these country patriots born?
To hunt and vote and raise the price of corn?

The poem which first established his fame, *Childe Harold's
Pilgrimage*, is notable among other things for its attacks on
such English national idols as Wellington. Byron's drinking
and debauchery and philandering were scandalous even by
the standards of Regency London; he was ostracized in polite
society and as soon as it became easy to travel, he spent most
of his time on the continent.

In *Childe Harold* he wrote:

I have not loved the world nor the world me.

Even so, in Switzerland or Mediterranean countries such as
Italy or Greece he was happy; and his later poems are rich
with evocations of nature as he had found it in southern
climes. Southern peoples also seemed to Byron to be agreeably
free from the hypocrisy which dominated his compatriots at
home. The cause of Greece appealed to him all the more
because of his liking for the Greeks – a liking which in the
case of his Greek page Loukas Chalandritsanos seems to have
exceeded the love he felt for any woman – and he entered the
struggle for Greek liberation with more enthusiasm than
prudence. In any case, Byron despised prudence:

Hereditary bondsmen! Know ye not
Who would be free themselves must strike the blow?

Other romantic poets might exemplify the man of feeling as
opposed to the man of reason. Byron presented himself to the
world as a man of action. He provided modern romanticism
with its model of the poet as hero.

He was none the less romantic for being a flawed hero. Just
as his club foot made him more rather than less physically
attractive to women, so did his reputation for immorality
merely add to his glamour. The Lake poets recoiled in horror –

'a monster' was Wordsworth's description of him; 'satanic' was Coleridge's word – but public disapproval was more than matched by public fascination. There was certainly little sympathy for those numerous women whose hearts were broken as a consequence of Byron's philandering. He wrote a long poem about all that entitled *Don Juan*, the story of Don Juan being the story of Byron himself, an exercise in confession without repentance. Byron's intervention in the liberation of Greece was ineffectual; he died of a fever before he could go into any battles. But that did not matter; with his portrait painted in the colourful uniform of the Greek resistance, he was every inch the soldier–poet in the service of freedom, which is how the world saw him and revered him. He did not need the memorial he was denied at Westminster Abbey for the simple reason that he was never to be forgotten – even his name became immortalized as an adjective almost synonymous with 'romantic': 'Byronic'.

Poetry is the art in which English romanticism found its best expression, if only because prose writers of the time remained for the most part creatures of the Enlightenment. Novelists, in the golden age of English romantic poetry, tended to be realists, adherents of the philosophy of Locke, observers of individuals and of society, champions of common sense and prudent self-interest against emotional excess and extravagance. Writers such as Jane Austen and Thomas Love Peacock chose to mock Gothic fiction rather than seek, with Mary Shelley, to create a serious literature of imagination. However, in the year 1847, an unknown schoolmistress in the North of England produced, shortly before her death at the age of thirty, a single book which is a masterpiece of romantic fiction – perhaps the most totally romantic novel in any language – *Wuthering Heights* by Emily Brontë. The basic plot is again that of *La nouvelle Héloïse*: a young lady (Cathy) falls in love with a young man (Heathcliff) who is her social inferior, and he loves her in return; instead of marrying him, however, she enters a sensible marriage with a suitor of her own class (Linton). The lover goes away, but when he returns years later, the heroine realizes that she has always loved him, and although she remains faithful to her husband, the emotional stress of reawakened feelings drives her to an early grave. There is much more intensity in *Wuthering Heights* than in *La nouvelle Héloïse*, and a wider range of passions. Emily Brontë's Heathcliff is not a philosopher like Rousseau's St-Preux, stoical in defeat. Heathcliff never forgives his Cathy for choosing Linton and he takes a terrible revenge on her husband and all her middle-class relations for the humiliations inflicted on him. The sphere of class conflict is not simply one degree lower – plebeian versus bourgeois as distinct from bourgeois versus aristocratic in Rousseau's story; the difference of class is more extreme and the conflict more impassioned. St-Preux, after all, is as cultured as Wolmar, and is unsuitable as a husband only in the eyes of Julie's snobbish father. Heathcliff, the orphan boy from the Liverpool slums is, by contrast, a kind of savage, still primitive and rough at the time of Cathy's marriage, and he only acquires a worldly polish when he goes off to make his fortune. In his *Discourse on Inequality* Rousseau had described how destructive passions arise at the same time as love in human experience: 'Jealousy awakens with love, discord triumphs and the sweetest of the passions receives sacrifices of human blood.' And yet in his *La nouvelle Héloïse*, Rousseau allows only noble feelings to inform the conduct of his characters. Emily Brontë is truer to Rousseau's own perception of human psychology. She shows how Heathcliff's bitterness at losing Cathy dominates, together with his love for Cathy, his whole life, even after her death. And although Cathy dies halfway through the novel, it loses none of its intensity because her spirit lives on, haunting Heathcliff as he exacts his vengeance on the world that has robbed him of her until finally his heart softens.

Emily Brontë explores more deeply the motivation of her characters than Rousseau does of his. She shows us her heroine divided, at the point of her marriage to Linton, by two sorts of love. 'My love for Linton is like the foliage of the woods: time will change it, I'm well aware, as winter changes the trees. My love for Heathcliff resembles the eternal rocks beneath . . . I am Heathcliff. He's always in my mind; not as a pleasure any more than I am always a pleasure to myself, but always in my own being.'

Only slowly does Cathy come to realize that in choosing the comfort and security of life with Linton she has chosen death. When Heathcliff returns to their Yorkshire village, a rich and powerful man, her mind becomes disturbed. She can neither live with him nor live without him. Instead of comforting her, he reproaches her: 'You loved me – what right had you to leave me?' When she dies, Heathcliff exclaims: 'I cannot live without my life, I cannot live without my soul.'

In the first half of the novel Heathcliff is a sympathetic character; after Cathy's death he becomes a monster as he sets about the ruin of Cathy's bourgeois family with hatred and systematic cruelty; and yet he never entirely loses the reader's sympathy; the badness in Heathcliff, like the badness in Byron, is part of what makes him a romantic hero, the romantic hero being, as we have noted, a flawed hero, and as such perhaps closer to the heroes of the real world than are the pure heroes of epic and classical mythology. The strangest thing about *Wuthering Heights* is that it was written by a clergyman's spinster daughter with very little personal experience of love or life, a triumph of the imagination – the imagination in Coleridge's sense of the power of insight into both the conscious and unconscious forces by which human behaviour is animated.

The greatest achievements of English romanticism were almost entirely literary. There were no notable English composers during the lifetime of Wordsworth – from 1770 to 1850 – and the painters of the period did not form a cohesive school. There was, however, one English painter who made a formidable contribution to romanticism in art: J. W. M. Turner. Other English painters of the period provided 'poetic' images of the landscape – Constable, Samuel Palmer and Richard Wilson for example; and there are heightened visionary qualities in the work of Blake and Fuseli; but Turner is unique in his contribution to the conquest of the sublime. He was inspired by the elements of fire and water, and endeavoured in his canvases to depict the force as well as the appearance of nature. He found new uses for colour; his evocation of both sunlight and moonlight are almost miraculous in their intensity. Without being at all metaphysical, Turner was as visionary as Blake. He prefigured the discoveries of the Impressionists, without ever losing the admiration of the critics of his own and succeeding generations.

One critic who was a contemporary, William Hazlitt, moderated his praise by complaining that Turner offered 'representations not properly of nature as of the medium through which they were seen'. This was precisely the originality of Turner: to have transcended the forms and literal meaning of his subjects in order to communicate the energy and force of nature through colour, texture and atmosphere. He travelled fairly extensively in search of sensational scenery. For Turner, as for Rousseau, the Alps were a source of particular inspiration: the glaciers, snow-capped peaks, forests, ravines, and waterfalls clothed in mists and cloud or illuminated by the glow of sunrise or sunset provided rich material for his paintings and he seldom failed to discern the sublime in the catastrophic, in *The Burning of Parliament* for example, *The Retreat of Napoleon from Russia*, *The Battle of the Nile* or *The Great Flood*. And yet Turner did not need a dramatic subject to impart drama to a scene, he achieved his visual effects by the diffusion of light and colour, capturing instead of the ordered serenity of Sir Joshua Reynolds' Newtonian universe, the fleeting fiery moments of Heraclitean flux.

4

French Romanticism

If romanticism had its first philosophers in Rousseau and Diderot, it did not flourish in France for several decades; rationalism and classicism were too deeply rooted in the national culture. The French Revolution rejected many traditions but it perpetuated and even strengthened the cult of reason. The earliest revolutionaries – Mirabeau, Lafayette, Condorcet – remained attached to the teachings of the Enlightenment; their immediate successors – Danton, Robespierre, St-Just – took as their model the ancient Roman republic and the Rousseau they invoked was the champion of classical virtue in *The Social Contract*, not the Romantic of *La nouvelle Héloïse*; Napoleon demanded a somewhat theatrical restatement of the aesthetics of the Roman Empire. Great artists, writers and musicians were noticeably few in number in revolutionary France. Although André Chénier is remembered as a poet of the Revolution who perished on the guillotine and thus became an icon of romantic martyrology, French romanticism found its best exponents among writers such as Chateaubriand who left France and opposed the Revolution. What returned to France when the migrants trickled back was a cosmopolitan romanticism to which Swiss, German, English, Scottish and Spanish influences contributed.

A key figure in this movement was Germaine de Staël. She
has been aptly described as the mistress of the age, not only
because she had affairs with most of the leading romantic
writers – Chateaubriand and Constant among them – but
because she wrote books that served as manifestos of the
romantic movement in its years of supremacy. Like Rousseau,
Mme de Staël was a Swiss and a Protestant. The wife of a
Swedish diplomat, she was also the daughter of the Genevese
financier Necker who became Louis XVI's most celebrated
and controversial minister. She established her credentials as
a Romantic with her very first book *Lettres sur Jean-Jacques
Rousseau* in 1788 and then went on to expound for French
readers the philosophy of romanticism as it was being developed by the literary critics and metaphysicians in Germany,
a subject she learned at first hand from August Wilhelm
Schlegel when he joined her household in Switzerland.

Her most influential publication was her book *De l'Allemagne*, where she described German literature and culture,
which she called 'romantic', and contrasted it favourably with
French literature and culture, which she called 'classical'. In
Germany, she argued, there were no fixed rules of taste;
everyone was allowed to judge a work of art for himself; to
judge it, moreover, according to the impression he received of
it and not according to pre-established rules. In Germany
there were no rules. A German author formed his public, she
said, while a French author was under the orders of his public.
German authors, being manifestly superior to their readers,
governed them, and felt no need to modify or moderate their
writings in order to please society as French authors did.
They let themselves go, even to extremes. Far from being
inhibited by laws of decorum, the German artists felt free to
express strong and vital emotions or deep and subtle thoughts.
And whereas the French public read books 'only to talk about
them in society', a German read for his personal satisfaction
alone, seeking 'in the silence of his retreat' an 'intimate

emotion'. Inwardness, she noted, was the quality the Germans prized. While the French exalted clarity as the first virtue of a writer, the Germans considered clarity a lesser merit; indeed the Germans felt entirely at home in the realm of shadows, obscurity, darkness. German authors, being looked upon as oracles, could envelop themselves in as many clouds as they wished. Style in general was less esteemed in Germany than the nobility of the thoughts and feelings expressed in art or literature.

In drama, Mme de Staël explained, the Germans assigned priority to action, to stirring events, to the display of violent passions, with the result that their plays were more effective on the stage than were the works of French dramatists. French poetry, she claimed, was so restricted by its adherence to rules that it had failed to develop as French society had developed since the sixteenth century. The true lyricists in France were the great prose writers, such as Bossuet and Fénelon. Mme de Staël carried her identification of romantic art with the Germanic art to the point of suggesting that those French authors who possessed similar romantic qualities, such as Rousseau, Bernardin de Saint-Pierre and Chateaubriand, 'belong to the Germanic school without knowing it' because 'they draw their talent from the depth of their souls'.

In the class 'Germanic', however, Mme de Staël made it clear that she included besides the Germans other northern cultures such as the English, who had refused to submit to the dead hand of classicism. The choice between romanticism and classicism, she insisted, was not a choice between two equally valid forms of modern art, but a choice between creation and imitation, between an original and a copy. What was called 'classical' in the present was really 'neo-classical'; it was a 'transplanted literature' from a dead age; it did not belong to the living world; romantic art did.

Mme de Staël's collaborator, compatriot and lover, Benjamin Constant, also argued in his *Réflexions sur la tragédie de*

Wallenstein that the German theatre afforded a model for French dramatists to follow, but having been partly educated in Scotland, Constant was even more responsive to the splendour of Shakespeare; he suggested that the adherence of French playwrights to the classical dogma of the unities in drama had prevented them bringing to the stage the flesh-and-blood characters of Shakespeare or his images of real life.

Both Mme de Staël and Constant were inevitably accused of attacking France's great cultural tradition and of promoting values that were alien and subversive. Indeed Napoleon had *De l'Allemagne* suppressed in 1810 after it had been published in England, and it did not appear in France until four years later. Mme de Staël had tried to show, however, that she was not advocating anything foreign to France, but was simply appealing to an older tradition which the French had once shared with the Germanic nations, to a world the French had lost, the medieval world of Christianity and chivalry and the spirit of the troubadours. Romantic art, she pointed out, took its standards from that world, just as classical art took its standards from the ancient world. The French alone, she argued, had cut themselves off from the medieval tradition since the Renaissance and had sought to revive artificially the pagan aesthetics of dead antiquity. It was classicism, she protested, which was the alien presence in a France which belonged to Christian Europe.

Neither Mme de Staël nor Constant, being Protestants, was well placed to stimulate a revival of medieval Christianity, which was, of course, Catholic Christianity. That mission was more fittingly assumed by Chateaubriand, who was Catholic, Breton, and noble, and who quickly established himself in exile as the leading French writer of the revolutionary period. Chateaubriand first appeared in print in 1797 as a critic of the various Protestant cults and sects which were then attracting intellectuals, but his criticisms were addressed from a sceptical rather than a Catholic perspective. His early novel

Atala seems even to mock Catholicism and its doctrine of absolution. It is another *roman de l'individu* in the style of *La nouvelle Héloïse*, but set in the forests of the New World, where the author had spent part of his exile from revolutionary France. The Red Indian heroine of *Atala* has taken a solemn vow to remain chaste, then falls passionately in love with a brave named Chactas. In order to avoid betraying her vow, she swallows poison. Dying, she declares to the beloved Chactas in the presence of a Catholic missionary: 'As I am about to enter Eternity and see with joy my virginity devour my life, I carry with me the sorrow of never having been yours.' The missionary reproves her: 'My daughter, your sorrow leads you astray . . . You could have been forgiven for a lapse from the vow of chastity.' His intervention has come too late. Atala dies, knowing that she might have been happy had she lived.

Chateaubriand, however, went on to write another *roman de l'individu* in a somewhat different spirit, *René*, which is about a young man whose alienation is due to his lack of religious faith. This story was incorporated in a longer work *Le Génie du christianisme*, which bears witness to Chateaubriand's reconversion to the Catholic church into which he had been baptized. He praises that ancestral faith for its beauty, for its power to heal human sorrow, for its rituals, for its contribution to art and architecture and, not least, for its service to freedom and peace.

Chateaubriand does not argue that Catholic doctrine is true, only that the Catholic religion is good, and especially good for sensitive souls who are conscious of the inevitable suffering of the human condition. Chateaubriand's faith in the church was like Rousseau's faith in Providence: it rested on an emotional need born of suffering: *'j'ai pleuré, j'ai prié, j'ai cru'*.

Le Génie du christianisme was published in 1802, a significant year in Napoleon's rise to power, but although Napoleon re-established the Catholic church, he was as unresponsive to religiosity as he was to romanticism. He was happy with neo-classical art and promoted it for propaganda purposes; seeing himself as the Caesar of the modern world, he decided that artists who accepted the disciplines of Roman aesthetics were those best fitted to express his vision and further his ambitions. He was, moreover, fortunate in having, at least in the visual arts, outstanding talents at his disposal. In such paintings as that by Jacques David representing the Emperor crowning himself and that by Ingres showing the Emperor enthroned, art and propaganda are magnificently fused, and even the more vulgarly theatrical scenes of imperial glory painted by lesser neo-classical practitioners such as Gros and Girodet are by no means undistinguished as paintings. Napoleon was doubly fortunate in the fact that despite his hostility to romanticism, romantic artists often admired him. The most famous example among musicians is that of Beethoven, who composed his 'Eroica' symphony in Napoleon's honour; while among French romantic writers, Balzac, Victor Hugo and Stendhal all fell, at one time or another, under Napoleon's spell; many more, in other countries, did so both in his lifetime and after his death.

Despite his attachment to neo-classical aesthetics, Napoleon was surely a romantic personality, indeed after a succession of romantic anti-heroes, he could be seen, at last, as a romantic hero, a man of humble origins rising by courage and strength of will to conquer a continent, and to do so, moreover, in the name of that supremely romantic ideal, liberty. That he committed crimes on the way and failed in the end in no way detracted from his romantic image, for neither crime nor failure is alien to romanticism; and if Napoleon felt himself best depicted in his lifetime by classical artists, his immortality in history and mythology (in so far as the two can be distinguished) was established by Romantics.

Among the first Romantics to respond to his charisma were Chateaubriand, Mme de Staël and Constant. Chateaubriand accepted a diplomatic appointment under Napoleon, only to break with him decisively a few months later when the Duc d'Enghien was executed on the Emperor's orders. Mme de Staël, who shared with her German mentors an admiration for power as intense as her love of liberty, returned to Paris soon after the Napoleonic *coup d'état*, opened a political salon there and pulled strings with her usual energy to secure for Benjamin Constant, her protégé, a place in Napoleon's Tribunate for the Department of Léman. But Napoleon soon lost patience with her interfering, bossy ways, and it was not long before he had her thrown out of France together with Constant. Back in Switzerland, the pair turned from politics to literature once more, and both chose that favourite romantic form, the *roman de l'individu*; she wrote *Delphine* and *Corinne*; he wrote *Adolphe*.

Mme de Staël's *Delphine* was often spoken of as 'a female *Werther*', doubtless because, in the original version, the novel ends with Delphine committing suicide. But the author did not intend her heroine to be a weakling like Goethe's protagonist; she visualized her as a woman of great strength of character, like herself, or at least as she saw herself, generous, trusting, passionate, virtuous and beautiful but unfortunate in loving a man of rigid conventionality who cared only for his reputation. When readers saw in Delphine's suicide a mark of weakness, Mme de Staël promptly rewrote the ending and had her heroine die instead of a broken heart.

Delphine is not a great novel; it encouraged an unfortunate tendency in future French romanticism to descend into melodrama. Mme de Staël's second novel *Corinne* is more restrained, but it succeeds rather as a travelogue about Italy than as a work of fiction. Constant's *Adolphe*, on the other hand, is a small masterpiece. The central character is the usual anti-hero; Adolphe, like Chateaubriand's René, knows that his estrangement from the world is due to the lack of religious faith, for without divine aid he cannot find the moral strength to do what he ought to do. What Adolphe cannot bring himself to do is break with Ellénore, a woman he has ceased to love, but who will not let him go. He cannot bear to hurt her, and so she keeps him, by bullying or moral blackmail, tied to her until a wretched death separates them. Miraculously Mme de Staël failed to see that *Adolphe* was the true story of Constant's life with her, and she believed him when he said of Ellénore, in whom everyone could see the spitting image of her despotic self, that it was the portrait of Anna Lindsay – an Irish woman with whom he had had an affair in Paris some years earlier.

Romanticism flourished in France under the Restoration of the legitimist Bourbon dynasty which followed the defeat of Napoleon at Waterloo. The new regime, having been imposed on the country by foreign armies, needed cultural support. Because Napoleon had exploited neo-classicism for his own ideological purposes, his successors looked for something different, for a clear-cut alternative to the rationalism which had propelled France through the errors of the Enlightenment to the excesses of the Revolution. Romanticism, it was thought, could perhaps serve this purpose, even though romanticism had already in other places shown that it could take a left- as well as a right-wing form. The legitimist regime therefore gave romanticism a hesitant, nervous approbation. Louis XVIII was an avowed patron of classical aesthetics, and all the public works in the way of architecture and sculpture commissioned by his government were in that style; the leading theoreticians of the Right, Joseph de Maistre and Louis de Bonald, demanded a return to the classical cultural standards as well as the political principles of the seventeenth century; anything *rousseauesque* was as hateful to them as anything *voltairien*. However, the Restoration was not intended to be a return to the absolutism of Louis XIV; it was meant to be based on a reconciliation between the crown and that nobility which Louis XIV had antagonized; and a nobility in the Restoration aiming to recover lost powers looked not to the seventeenth century, but rather to the earlier precedent of that medieval, feudal France which romanticism glorified. Thus in the earliest years of the Restoration, romanticism found favour with several of the leading aristocratic and clerical elements in the government, despite the King's antipathy.

Chateaubriand was the first romantic writer to rally to the legitimist regime, and the last to forsake it. He was made a viscount at the Restoration and took an active part as a conservative in the politics of the next fifteen years. Constant was equally active as a liberal. In 1815 the political differences between French romantics were not great. Conservatives and liberals were alike in their attachment to moderation. There was at this stage no hint of that yearning for excess which already characterized some forms of German romanticism; indeed there was a perceptible shrinking from violence after all the bloodshed of the revolutionary Terror and the Napoleonic wars. Chateaubriand's conservatism was not far removed from that of Montesquieu, and although he attached a greater value to the Catholic church, he had the same faith in constitutional government and divided sovereignty as instruments of liberty. Constant's liberalism was correspondingly close to that of Locke, and he sought to lead progressive opinion away from the extreme democratic concept of freedom which the Revolution had derived from Rousseau – the concept of freedom as the collective exercise of a nation ruling itself. Instead, Constant pleaded for an individualistic notion of freedom, which was the only one he believed appropriate to the modern world, freedom understood as each man having the right to do whatever he pleased so long as it was lawful.

With Chateaubriand in the House of Peers and Constant in the Chamber of Deputies, romantic writers might almost seem to have become incorporated into the political Establishment. But what about their artistic production? Novels like *Delphine*, *Adolphe* and *Atala* could hardly serve to awaken respect for the Catholic church, the traditional order of monarchy, nobility and clergy, or the values of chivalry and family, let alone reawaken the spirit of the troubadours. Romanticism triumphed in the visual arts after 1815, but the impact of the greatest paintings was hardly more conducive to the aims of the regime. The most impressive canvases of Géricault and Delacroix are those which depict defeat, not victory. Géricault's *Le Radeau de la Méduse* shows shipwrecked passengers on a raft crying in vain to be rescued by a passing frigate; the same artist's paintings of war introduce more vanquished than victorious soldiers. Delacroix's *Scènes des massacres de Scio* represents Greek men, women and children being murdered by Turks, and his *La Mort de Sardanapule* shows the Assyrian king preparing for suicide while his slaves constrain his concubines to die with him. Such paintings were inevitably disturbing rather than reassuring to the subjects of the Restoration monarchy.

The romantic poets proved for a time better servants of the legitimist ideology, especially the young men associated with *La Muse française*, a royalist and religious group which included Lamartine, Vigny and Victor Hugo. Lamartine, twenty-two years younger than Chateaubriand, was the oldest of them and also the most devout; each in his own way proclaimed the need for religious institutions as well as for a monarchy and an aristocracy; and their poems were all on suitably elevated, sacred and sometimes even Biblical themes.

Lamartine first earned fame in 1820 with his *Méditations poétiques*. These poems were inspired by the death of his mistress, yet he succeeded in transforming feelings of private grief into thoughts about universal suffering. He produced verse of great lyrical beauty, in a style at once musical and dialectical. Technically, Lamartine was the most original of poets, but his innovations were meant to be more than technical; they were intended to revolutionize poetry by giving it sincerity. In later life he claimed that he had been 'the first to bring poetry down from Parnassus, and instead of drawing sounds from the strings of the lyre, to draw them from the very fibres of the human heart.'

Lamartine's attachment to the church lasted until the death in 1829 of his mother, and evidently having owed much to her influence, did not long outlive her. His next important collection of poems *Harmonies poétiques* still contains many verses on spiritual subjects, but gives expression as much to doubt as to faith, and includes a 'Hymne au Christ' which combines adoration of the saviour with bitter criticism of the church. A journey to the Holy Land in the 1830s, far from restoring Lamartine to Catholic obedience, left him with little religious faith beyond a vague mystical deism.

Vigny's religious beliefs were minimal from the start. His attachment to the ideology of the Restoration was that of a strong believer in monarchy and an even stronger believer in aristocracy. The religion to which he subscribed he once spoke of as 'la Religion de l'Honneur' – a 'male religion, without symbols, images, dogmas or rites'. If he was ever ready to admit the existence of God, it was only to say that God was cruel rather than loving. Vigny often asserted that the history of the church was a history of persecutions. Nevertheless he accepted the necessity of a religious institution to uphold morality among the people, more especially in an age when the elevating influence of the nobility and its code of honour had effectively been lost as a result of the Revolution.

Vigny was never a sceptic in the cheerful spirit of the Enlightenment, but a man tormented by religious problems. The book entitled *Poèmes*, which came out in 1822, and the successive collections of verse which appeared throughout the decade, all revolve around moral themes, many set in historical or biblical contexts. Even when the union of the sensual and the spiritual is most skilfully accomplished, Vigny's poetry betrays a troubled and divided personality.

It fell to Victor Hugo, the youngest poet attached to *La Muse française*, to explain the particular connection they believed to exist between romanticism and Christianity. He did so in the preface to his play *Cromwell*. In these pages Hugo pointed out that romanticism had learned from Christianity a great truth, namely the truth about the double nature of man. In the light of the doctrines of the creation and the fall, man was revealed by Christianity to be at once both evil and good, part angel part beast. This was an insight which the philosophers of classical antiquity did not have, with the result that classical aesthetics, like classical ethics, insisted on the total separation of good and evil, of beauty and ugliness, of darkness and light, of truth and falsehood. Christian philosophy, by contrast, opened the mind to the possibility of a synthesis of opposites, and romantic art attempted to explore both the sublime and the grotesque. Such antitheses were in nature and were also in those great masters of literature which the neo-classical critics despised – Dante, Cervantes and Shakespeare. The best poetry, Hugo declared, was to be found '*dans l'harmonie des contraires*'.

Romantic poetry in France acknowledged a particular debt to Shakespeare. Guizot published in 1820 his *Shakespeare et son temps* to recommend the Elizabethan and Jacobean drama to French readers; Stendhal in 1823 argued in his *Shakespeare et Racine* that the author of *Hamlet* was in most respects superior to the author of *Phèdre*; Vigny overcame the hostility to Shakespeare of the Théâtre-Français by translating *Othello* for performance there, and Musset took Shakespeare as his model in his most successful play *Lorenzaccio*. Nevertheless Shakespeare had always to be forced down the throats of the French public. The writer they took to instantly without any prompting from the critics was Walter Scott, and his influence on romanticism in France was prodigious.

Walter Scott was to all appearances the typical *bon bourgeois* of Edinburgh, a successful lawyer who collected Scottish ballads as a hobby, and published a set in volume form. He was the kind of man who had done well out of the political union of Scotland with England and the economic prosperity which the industrial revolution had brought to the middle classes of the Lowlands. However, his interest in folklore opened his eyes to another Scotland, the Scotland of the Highland clans that had rallied to Prince Charles in 1745 and attempted by marching south against the unionist forces of George I to restore the independence of Scotland and the reign of the Scottish House of Stuart. It was, of course, a doomed enterprise, and the defeat of Prince Charles's troops at Culloden restored tranquillity to the ancient Scottish kingdom as a British province, dedicated to the ethos of Presbyterian utility, piety, thrift and work. Against this grey consummation, the minstrel in Walter Scott, the collector of ballads in which the voice of an older Scotland spoke, rebelled, and he set about writing novels in which that voice might be heard anew. In the first of these novels, *Waverley*, published in the last year of Napoleon's power in France, Scott sought to relate the true narrative of the Highlands' last rebellion in the form of fiction. His purpose as a historical novelist was, he explained, to explore 'the characters and passions of the actors — those passions common to men in all stages of society and which have alike agitated the human heart whether it throbbed under the steel corselet of the fifteenth century, the brocaded coat of the eighteenth, or the blue frock and white dimity waistcoat of the present day.'

The success of *Waverley*, and the series of historical novels that Scott wrote thereafter, astonished him. They appealed to the new reading public that universal education generated in France where their popularity exceeded that in the British Isles. In Scotland itself, Scott's novels prompted Lowlanders to invent tartans for their families, to wear kilts and listen to the bagpipes, and find all the ways they could to assert their identity as Scotsmen. But Scott's novels did not provoke in

Scotland the kind of nationalism which romanticism promoted elsewhere. They generated nostalgia without deep
discontent. His Scottish readers were too conscious of the
material advantages of the union of their kingdom with England to wish for secession. Scott's romanticism was essentially
a conservative romanticism. Edward, the hero of *Waverley*,
ends up much as Scott himself ended up – satisfied to adventure in thought while enjoying comfort in life. The Jacobite
heroine, Flora, predicts rather mournfully of Edward, that 'he
will refit the old library in the most exquisite Gothic taste,
and garnish its shelves with the rarest and most valuable
volumes; and he will draw plans and landscapes, and will
write verses and raise temples, and dig grottoes, and he will
stand on a clear summer night in the colonnade before the
hall, and gaze on the deer as they stray in the moonlight . . .
and he will repeat verses to his beautiful wife, who will hang
upon his arm, and he will be a happy man.'

Scott's novels were designed to nourish the fantasies of his
readers without disturbing them; and in the English-speaking
world they had the desired effect. In France the impact was
more unsettling. If the French public ignored Mme de Staël's
command to read the German authors, they feasted on those
who wrote in English, and Walter Scott headed the list.
Beginning in 1816 his novels were speedily translated into
French, and a sixty-volume edition of his works, published in
the 1820s, sold no less than one and a half million copies in
six years. Under the spell of Walter Scott, French writers
introduced history into literature and French scholars introduced romanticism into history.

Augustin Thierry, one of the greatest historians of the
time, said there was more 'true history' in Scott's *Ivanhoe* than
in the work of most historians, and Scott's influence on Thierry's
own work is obvious. His *Histoire de la conquête de l'Angleterre
par les Normands* is full of the same sort of colour and movement as Scott's novels. Even as a schoolboy at Blois, Thierry

had imagined himself taking part in the battles of the Franks and Gauls. But he combined imagination with scholarship, and all his historical writings were based on diligent research in archives. In articles he wrote for *Le Courrier français* he declared his commitment to a 'new history' which would not simply relate the doings of kings, warriors and other great personalities, but record the events of everyday life and describe the experiences of the common man. Thierry was a liberal, and he warned readers against the hidden ideological content of what still passed for history in France: books that made the history of the conquest of the Gauls by the Franks the history of the nation, for such a picture of events, he argued, supported the claims of the nobility to political supremacy. In his *Histoire de la conquête de l'Angleterre*, Thierry showed the Britons succeeding where the Gauls had failed, in recovering their ancient rights, and in his *Lettres sur l'histoire de France* he went on to argue that the resistance of the conquered Gauls against the conquering Franks had persisted down the ages in the struggles of French commoners against French noblemen.

This sympathy for the people, envisaged as the true subjects of history, was even more intense in the writings of Thierry's contemporary Jules Michelet. He, too, thrilled at an early age to the magic of the past; he once described how, as a small boy, he had gazed on the 'pale faces' of the medieval sculptures in Museum of French Monuments in Paris and yearned to learn more about the spirit of those distant times. Of the twenty years he spent in the Royal Archives, Michelet said that in that 'profound silence' murmurs reached his ears, a sound which was not the voice of the dead, but that of living, speaking beings. Joan of Arc had heard voices, and Jules Michelet heard Joan of Arc: he depicted her not only as the saviour of the French but as the virgin mother leading them to become a single entity. France, he declared, was *'une personne'*. Putting foward an idea which was later elaborated

by Hegel, Michelet suggested that it was by fighting a war –
a war against the English under the inspiration of Joan of Arc
– that the French people achieved consciousness of themselves as a nation. Against the royalist belief that the kings of
France made France by uniting the people as their subjects,
Michelet insisted that the people themselves made France,
and in his book *Le Peuple* and other writings he presented the
people as heroes of a great collective adventure, the details of
which he described with a sense of excitement that took the
reader by the throat.

Thierry and Michelet wrote romantic history; and even
Guizot, the most eminent historian of their generation, was
affected by romanticism. In his book on Shakespeare, he
defended romantic literature; his historical writings combine
literature with scholarship, and unite the narrative and analytic methods no less effectively than do Thierry's; but Guizot did not have a romantic personality. A pious Protestant
who had been educated in Geneva, he was at once too ambitious and too prudent, too buttoned-up and conventional, too
frightened of extremes in any form, to allow imagination the
freedom that romanticism demanded. He nevertheless played
a decisive role politically, in promoting an alliance between
liberals and Romantics, in opposition to Chateaubriand's
alliance of conservatives and Romantics.

Scott's influence on the authors of novels and plays matched
that he exercised on historians, and can be measured by the
extent to which the most illustrious Romantics turned from
romans de l'individu to writing historical works with a large
cast: Hugo's *Notre Dame de Paris*, for example, Vigny's *Cinq-
Mars*, Gauthier's *Le Capitaine Fracasse* and Balzac's *Les Chouans*.
Vigny's *Cinq-Mars*, however, departs from Scott's model in
one important respect: it introduces real historical person-
ages, rather than fictional characters, as the central figures.
Moreover Vigny's *Cinq-Mars* is an undisguised *pièce à thèse*:
it represents Cinq-Mars as the hero of the struggle of the

French nobility against Richelieu's policy of transforming the crown of France into an absolute monarchy. Vigny's play about the English poet *Chatterton*, shows that his nostalgia for the feudal past was accompanied by an equally strong disapproval of the capitalist present; he used a dramatist's licence in presenting relationships between Chatterton and his landlord and landlady for which no historical evidence could be produced; but the play was a great success – paradoxically with the very bourgeois public whose values it was designed to attack.

Hugo's historical works were written on a grander scale. *Cromwell*, *Hernani* and *Marion de Lorme* were meant to be the romantic equivalent of the great verse dramas of seventeenth-century classicism, although it must be said that they more readily recall the libretto of an opera – long slabs of poetry stretched, like arias and recitatives, along the framework of a none too plausible plot.

Indeed opera itself was propelled into new channels by the example of Walter Scott. Boïeldieu's greatest success at the Paris opera was *La Dame blanche*, which came straight from Scott. The foreign musicians who dominated Paris musical life – Rossini and Meyerbeer – were hardly less responsive to the same vision of the romance of history. Most successful operas performed for the first time in Paris between 1826 and 1836 – Meyerbeer's *Robert le Diable*, *Les Huguenots*, Rossini's *Guillaume Tell*, *Moïse*, Auber's *Gustave III* and *La Muette de Portici* – were costume dramas about sensational clashes of passion in history, and their popularity with Paris audiences signalled the wholehearted acceptance of romanticism by middle-class taste, or at least the acceptance of romanticism in its middlebrow forms. The more highbrow romantic music of Berlioz, regarded today as the greatest French composer of his time, received a cool welcome from the public when it was first performed. His *Symphonie fantastique* and other works in which passions as strong as those in *Wuthering Heights* are given disturbing expression, were condemned at the time as '*la musique du fou*'.

During the fifteen years of the legitimist Restoration in France, romanticism changed its political complexion. While Louis XVIII was on the throne, romanticism may well have propped up the regime, for there were more conservatives than liberals among the Romantics. After the accession of Charles X there was a decisive swing to the Left. Various explanations have been suggested for this, but it is evident that the new king antagonized many people from the moment of his coronation at Rheims, in which a grandiose show of pageantry appeared to proclaim the advent of another absolute monarch in the style of Louis XIV. Charles X alienated writers and intellectuals even more when his government introduced a law which imposed both censorship and heavy taxation on the Press. Romanticism as a movement became increasingly subversive.

Some works were critical mainly of the social order. An example of this is Dumas's play *Antony*, in which the central character is a man of illegitimate birth, rejected for that reason as a suitor for the heroine who loves him. The play is an attack on prevailing prejudices against bastardy and to some extent an attack as well on the institution of marriage itself. Marriage is also the target of Musset's *André del Sarto*, in which the rights of a lover are asserted forcefully against those of a husband: love itself confers the right, claims Musset's Cordiani: 'I love and I am loved'. He will accept no more compelling argument.

Romantics also began to turn against the clergy. Lamennais, for example, had earned literary fame in 1817 with his *Essai sur l'indifférence en matière de Religion* in which he pleaded in language both tender and prophetic for a return to obedience to the church. However, he made it increasingly clear that by the church he meant the historic universal church founded by St Peter at Rome, and not the Gallican establishment of Restoration France, 'where religious jobs are like government jobs'. Lamennais is to be placed among the Romantics not only in virtue of his poetic style, but by reason of his attempt to dissociate Catholic faith from its traditional adherence to Thomistic rational philosophy and base it on the simple revelation of God's presence in the heart of every man. The more the Gallican bishops and the legitimist government attacked Lamennais's books, and persecuted the author, the more he moved to the Left, becoming in effect a Christian socialist of an increasingly radical persuasion. Thus a writer who had once been among the most eloquent champions of the Catholic church in France ended up as an anti-clerical republican who idealized only the workers, allying himself with Michelet and others in a new cult of *le peuple*. Sainte-Beuve wrote in 1830: 'People and poets are marching together. Art is henceforth on a popular footing, in the arena with the masses, side by side with tireless humanity.'

One of the swiftest transformations from Right to Left was that of Hugo. In 1824 he spoke of literature as 'the expression of a religious and monarchical society' and, as late as October 1826, he wrote: 'It is well understood that liberty does not mean anarchy'. But in February 1827 Hugo published a poem 'Hymne à la Colonne' which proclaims his adherence to liberalism, and in the preface to *Hernani* he went on to state his position in prose:

> Romanticism, taken as a whole, is only liberalism in literature. Literary liberalism will be no less democratic than political liberalism. Freedom in art and liberty in society are the twin goals to which all consistent and logical thinkers should march in step. The *ultras* of every kind, classicists or monarchists, will struggle in vain if they attempt to restore the *ancien régime* unchanged.

There can be little doubt that the Romantics did much to turn French opinion against the government of Charles X and towards the Revolution of 1830. But that was not a romantic revolution. There is a celebrated painting by Delacroix entitled 'July 28: Liberty leading the people' which depicts a half-naked female figure brandishing a flag, surrounded by a motley group of the Parisian crowd, some armed ones advancing, some fallen. As an allegorical scene it is more false than true. It is true in the sense that the population of Paris took up arms against the monarchy of Charles X on 28 July 1830. Eighteen hundred insurgents were killed and 4,500 wounded; and although only two hundred soldiers were killed and four hundred wounded, the King, seeing that he was beaten, abdicated. Even so, it was not a people's victory as much as a victory for the middle classes of France, and the leader of the Revolution was not bare-breasted Liberty but a top-hatted minister of the parliamentary centre, who produced as an alternative both to the absolutism which Charles X represented and the republicanism which the Paris populace demanded, a compromise in the person of the Duke of Orleans, a sovereign who was willing, when enthroned as Louis-Philippe, to accept 'the sovereignty of the nation' and allow a parliament elected by the rich to govern in its name. That minister was Guizot, the unlovable little Huguenot, who exploited the alliance between liberalism and romanticism to promote himself to the highest office at the expense of both liberalism and romanticism.

There were some Romantics who had no illusions at all about the July Revolution. Chateaubriand remained loyal to the overthrown Charles X. Stendhal, who is remembered as the greatest prose novelist of his generation, and whose *Shakespeare Racine et* of 1823 was one of the more impressive manifestos of romantic aesthetics, remained a Bonapartist in his heart and had only scorn for Louis-Philippe. Stendhal had formed a deep attachment to Italy during his military service there, and spent the years between 1814 and 1821 in Milan, happy to be away from Louis XVIII's France. A modest consular job in Civitavecchia after 1831 kept him no less contentedly away from the France of Louis-Philippe. In novels which included *La Chartreuse de Parme* and *Le Rouge et le noir* Stendhal developed the anti-hero of earlier romantic novelists into something approaching a hero: a young man who is aristocratic without being an aristocrat, who loves passionately but whose love is his misfortune, an outsider who disrupts the society from which he is alienated. Stendhal's *Vie de Napoléon*, published in 1829 helped, with Walter Scott's nine-volume biography, to establish the banished Emperor as another kind of hero in the imagination of French readers at just the time that Louis-Philippe and Guizot were instituting the decidely unromantic rule of 'middlingness'. Stendhal was, however, like Berlioz, too highbrow an artist to achieve due recognition in his lifetime, and he died in 1842 with nineteen of his thirty-three books unpublished, among them *Lucien Leuwen*, a piercing critique of the corruption that prevailed in France after the Revolution of 1830.

Most French Romantics, however, had greeted that revolution with enthusiasm. Hugo's vision of the events of 28 July was entirely in accord with Delacroix's picture of Liberty leading the insurgents, except that he would have made a poet the symbol of liberty; a poet to march *'devant les peuples comme une lumière et leur montrer le chemin'*. Hugo was content to serve the cause of liberty as a writer. Lamartine, on the other hand, turned from literature to practical politics. He stood successfully for the Chamber of Deputies in 1833 and, as he moved further and further to the left, became the effective leader of the provisional government after the Revolution of 1848 against Louis-Philippe had instituted a republic. In a somewhat similar fashion to Lamennais, Lamartine seems to have found in socialism a substitute for his lost faith in Catholic Christianity. Indeed it could be said that before the introduction of scientific socialism by Marx, socialism was itself a creation of the romantic imagination – an imagination stirred by compassion for the plight of the poor in a world increasingly dominated by the harsh entrepreneurial ethos of nineteenth-century industrialization.

The years between 1815 and 1852 were kind to the French Romantics. The very instability of the three successive monarchies, the insecurities of a society no longer held together by habit, custom and tradition seem to have called forth the creative powers of the imagination, and prompted artists to feel themselves free both to produce whatever art they chose and called upon to enact the role of the 'legislators of mankind'. As legislators they were not in France as in Shelley's famous line, 'unacknowledged', but, on the contrary, very widely recognized, respected and esteemed, with more authority over the hearts and minds of their contemporaries than the politicians in parliament. The year 1852 which introduced the reign of technology and vulgarity with that of Napoleon III, marked the end of this era, but not the end of romanticism in France. It survived, however, in the interstices rather than the forefront of the national culture, in part assimilated by movements which were superficially opposed to it, in part eclipsed only to reappear in various guises in twentieth-century art.

5

Italian Romanticism

The first romantic writing in Italy was produced by a classi-
cist, Ugo Foscolo, who had made his name with verse translations from the Latin and had been appointed a university
professor of classical rhetoric at the age of twenty. He is
recognizably the Romantic in some of his early poems and in
a novel – yet another *roman de l'individu* – called *Jacopo Ortis*;
in both he is also a recognizably Italian Romantic in that he
expresses not only imagination and feeling but also a distinctive form of patriotic fervour, at once noble and melancholy.

In the novel, which is given the epistolary form of *La
nouvelle Héloïse* and *Werther*, Foscolo's central character Jacopo
is an impoverished young man, exiled by the Napoleonic
police from his native Venice to a village in the Euganean
hills where he meets and falls in love with Teresa, who turns
out to be betrothed to another, richer man. Feeling he can
offer nothing to compete with the fortune of his rival, Jacopo
goes off to wander around Italy, only to observe and lament
the wretched condition of the country under Napoleon's rule.
In Ravenna, he learns that Teresa has married her fiancé.
Impelled by a desire at least to see her once more, Jacopo pays
a last visit to the Euganean hills. In the night he writes a long
letter to Teresa declaring his feelings to her; next morning he
is found dead with a dagger in his heart. Sexual love is the

dominant passion in this novel, expressed as something both ardent and pure; but mixed with it is another passion, love for the Italy which has been conquered and betrayed by the French. Although the story ends in suicide, and the Italians are depicted as the pitiful victims of aggression, despair is not what is suggested or evoked by the novel so much as a sense of the permanence of love and the mutability of circumstance. The Italian nationalist leader Mazzini said he had learned Foscolo's novel by heart as a boy and never ceased to draw inspiration from it.

In Foscolo's poetry, patriotic sentiments are no less power-fully expressed. '*I Sepolcri*', for example, was written in protest against Napoleon's edict of 1806, forbidding the burial of the dead in churches in Italy. In these lines Foscolo depicts the tombs as precious symbols of the continuity between past and present. Like Edmund Burke, he dwells on the moral impor-tance in the life of a nation of the bonds which tie the living to the dead and to the generations yet to be born. Hope is more explicit in '*I Sepolcri*' than in *Jacopo Ortis*, in that the tombs are visualized not simply as monuments to illustrious Italians departed but as dark recesses from which a national resurrection may emerge; there is an early intimation here of what came to be known as the *Risorgimento*.

Unfortunately, Foscolo's own hopes of national resurgence and liberation were shattered in 1815, when Napoleonic despotism was ended only to be succeeded by Austrian des-potism; rather than submit to this, Foscolo chose to spend the last twelve years of his life in exile in England. The custody of romanticism in Italy passed at this stage to the literary critics. Once again the ubiquitous figure of Mme de Staël appeared on the scene. In January, 1816, the first issue of the journal *Biblioteca italiana* carried an article by her, ostensibly on the subject of translation, but in substance an attack on the classical aesthetics which, despite the innovations of Fos-colo, was still dominant in Italy; Mme de Staël added a plea for romanticism along the lines of the one she had addressed to the French.

The *Biblioteca italiana* was edited by a friend of Mme de Staël's, Giuseppe Acerbi. Unknown to its contributors, the journal was liberally financed by the imperial government in Vienna with the aim of countering the French influence over Italian culture which the defeat of Napoleon had not wholly eliminated, and restoring the hegemony of Austria. Since Napoleon had favoured neo-classicism, the *Biblioteca italiana* was at first allowed to attack that form of aesthetics, while romanticism, regarded as something Germanic, was guardedly welcomed by those who sought to bring Italian culture closer to that of a German-speaking empire.

There was, then, on the face of it, nothing in Mme de Staël's article to offend Vienna or hinder its appearance in the *Biblioteca italiana*. She did not repeat the argument set forth in *De la littérature* in 1800 that the decadence of Italian art and literature was due to the absence of freedom in a country which had languished since the Renaissance under the oppression of alien governments and the suffocating tutelage of the counter-Reformation church. Instead, she reproached Italian writers for their provincialism and conservatism, for their failure to translate into Italian the living, modern works which were being written in other languages, such as German and English. She criticized them sharply for their lack of originality, for continuously imitating past models, for cultivating a verbose, rhetorical, pompous style which did nothing to mitigate the monotony of their verses. Enslaved by what they considered to be the laws of classical poetics, the Italian authors were producing, she asserted, 'the poetry of words and sounds devoid of thought and meaning'.

Mme de Staël had agreed to write this article on a visit to Italy in 1815. On an earlier visit to the peninsula in 1804–5 in the company of August Wilhelm Schlegel and the Swiss historian Jean-Charles Sismondi, she had taken a great liking to the country, as is evident from the novel which that visit inspired, *Corinne*. The experience modified her conception of romanticism as 'northern', and she began to look for its origins not only in the Germanic Middle Ages, in Celtic and Nordic sagas, in Shakespeare and 'Ossian', but also in Mediterranean sources. Sismondi introduced her to Spanish literature, of which she had hitherto been almost totally ignorant, and suggested to her that it had almost always been 'romantic'. When Schlegel agreed with this, she began to think of romanticism as something 'southern'. In thinking in this way, Mme de Staël followed not only Chateaubriand and the French Catholic Romantics but her fellow Swiss Protestant, Rousseau, who found, as we have seen, some inspiration for his romanticism in the music of Italian composers, and who argued in his writings on language that the South gave birth to languages as poetry while the North originated languages merely as signals of utility. Rousseau conjectured that in southern climes where human needs were adequately furnished by nature, primitive men and women sang to another before they spoke to another. Southern languages, being prompted by passions, were melodic and lyrical, he suggested, from their beginnings while in the cold, harsh North, languages were introduced as instruments of communication between individuals who needed to co-operate in the struggle against scarcity. The first words of Southern man, said Rousseau, were 'love me'; of Northern man 'help me'; and thus the South became the birthplace of poetry and the North the birthplace of industry.

The French historian Michelet always regarded Italy as the birthplace of the romantic philosophy of history on the grounds that its true originator was Giabattista Vico, who was born in Naples in 1668 and taught at the university there until his death in 1744. Vico's books were neglected in Italy, but they were taken up after his death by Herder and others in Germany, so that what was generally considered an essentially German movement of thought derived, Michelet suggested, from the work of a Neapolitan professor. Here, then, to add to Lutheran pietism was an important element in the ancestry of romanticism, a southern element. In his various writings Vico disputed the claim put forward equally by the Italian rationalists of the seventeenth century and the *illuministi* of the Enlightenment in the eighteenth century that science could provide a comprehensive knowledge of reality. Science, he argued, could only produce knowledge of the material external world which God had made. Knowledge of what men had made – including knowledge of man himself, both inwardly and socially, in his communities and activities and institutions – could be acquired only by the study of man's history. By history, Vico explained, he meant not only past events, but all the arts, the languages, the myths and fables which expressed men's endeavours to understand their experience. He went on to suggest that while scientific knowledge might be acquired by observation and calculation, the other kind of knowledge could be gained only by an exercise of the imagination, which was needed to capture modes of experience beyond commonplace perception. Vico was thus not only an early champion of history against the indifference or hostility of the scientists, he set the agenda for the romantic school of historians which came into existence some years after his death.

Mme de Staël herself, as she came to know Italy better, discovered further elements of romanticism in Italy's own cultural history, and she suggested to her Italian readers that their obsession with the glories of ancient Rome and the achievements of the Renaissance was blinding them to the creative resources of other ages in Italian history, including the living present. Classicism was reducing Italy to the artistic nourishment of 'imitations of imitations'.

Her article provoked a vigorous controversy, such that even the Austrian authorities had second thoughts about it. The

proposal to translate German authors into Italian would seem
from their point of view to be a good one; but had not the
German Romantics already generated forms of nationalism
inimical to Austrian imperialism, and might not Italian romanticism do the same in Italy? In the event it did. In spite
of being attacked as something alien and unpatriotic by the
champions of Italian classicism, romanticism from the moment of its appearance in Italian poetry in the work of Foscolo
was put to the service of nationalism.

The *Biblioteca italiana*, having provided a platform for Mme
de Staël, quickly turned to provide one for her critics. Her
supporters, however, found other outlets, and Italy became as
rich in theorists of romanticism as in exponents of romantic
art. Italian romanticism was swift to define its own distinctive character. Not only was it patriotic, it was more Christian, more Catholic, than most other forms of romanticism; at
the same time it was less conservative than the Christian
romanticism of Chateaubriand and Coleridge, less metaphysical than the German romanticism of the Schlegels and
Fichte; and more of a coherent movement than romanticism
in England.

The very fact of living under the watchful eye of the Austrian censors prompted the Italian champions of romanticism
to ally themselves together as an ideological if not a political
group. Excluded from the *Biblioteca italiana*, they started a
journal of their own, which they called *Il Conciliatore*. Several
of them also published essays which came to be known as the
manifesti of Italian romanticism. The first of these critics, a
friend of Mme de Staël's named Ludovico di Breme, published his *Discorso* at his own expense in June, 1816, after it
had been rejected by the *Biblioteca italiana*. It was followed by
Piero Borsieri's *Avventurie letterarie* and Giovanni Berchet's
Lettera semiseria, both published in Milan. In his *Discorso* Di
Breme defended Mme de Staël's case for romanticism against
those authors who maintained that she was trying to impose

an alien culture on the Italians. He sought to disentangle loyalty to Italy from loyalty to a worn-out cultural tradition, which was itself disfigured by subservience to foreign rulers and by national disunity. Di Breme argued that true patriotism must prove itself by looking to the future rather than the past. He offered his readers a vision of Italy as a nation waiting to be born, existing in that faculty to which romanticism appealed, the imagination of its people.

Di Breme also defended the romantic ideal of nature, and argued that poetry should be 'impulsive, spontaneous and free', just as nature was. Since man was a part of nature, exploration of the self could lead to a greater knowledge of nature. Instead of the study of ancient mythology, to which Italian poets of the classical tradition were so dedicated, Di Breme suggested that they should investigate the passions which hold the key to human nature. At the same time he insisted that romanticism had no quarrel with the classics, but only with the neo-classicists. The revaluation of the ancient world by the Renaissance had been fruitful at the time because it had led to the emulation of noble models, but what had followed in the next three centuries had been a series of copies of copies. Aping had taken the place of emulation, which was itself an excellent practice, one which could well be extended, he added with an eye to Mme de Staël's argument for translations, from dead poets to foreign ones.

Di Breme named Byron as one such foreign poet, and, with Byron in focus, went on to describe the poet as 'a man who is active in the life of his own times and possessed with a sense of mission.' Di Breme did not specify that mission, but given Byron's known devotion to the cause of national liberation, Di Breme did not need to.

Mme de Staël died in 1817, but she lived long enough to read Di Breme's defence of her views, and she expressed her gratitude in a paragraph which was cut out by the censor from the second article she wrote for the *Biblioteca italiana*. Her other supporters, Borsieri and Berchet, succeeded in circumventing the censorship by presenting their arguments in the form of fiction or fantasy: the full title of Borsieri's essay was *Avventure letterarie di un giorno* (*One Day's Literary Adventures*), that of Berchet *Lettera semiseria de Grisostomo al suo figliuolo* (*Chrysostom's Half-serious Letter to his Son*). Thus disguised, Borsieri mocked the champions of the classical tradition as pedants, 'cardboard statues in a museum of antiquities'. Poetry, he argued, should not be an academic exercise, but an attempt to reveal some part of the mysteries of heaven and earth, and console human beings for the brevity of their anxious lives. Borsieri described the mission of poetry as 'speaking to the hearts and minds of educated readers'. But he also pleaded for a revaluation of popular folkloric literature, such as dialect verse, which he suggested might help the Italian people to understand each other more completely and so acquire a deeper national consciousness. He did not subscribe, with the German Romantics, to the ideal of the genius: on the contrary he suggested that Italian culture gave too much attention to the geniuses of the past, to the great figures of the Renaissance whose magnificence dwarfed the innumerable lesser talents in Italian art and held later generations spellbound. He believed that excessive veneration of the Leonardos and Raphaels was what had impelled Italian artists to try to imitate them, instead of developing their own creative powers, powers that needed to be set free from the constraints of academic legislators if they were to prove their worth.

Giovanni Berchet in his *Lettera semiseria* pleaded for freedom in art in terms which could even more readily be translated into a plea for freedom in politics. He envisaged the emergence of what he called a 'common literary fatherland' in Italy, suggesting that writers were at the same time citizens of the world and members of a particular group which was constituted by a shared language. Towards that particular

group, he added, writers had a special responsibility as custo-
dians of the language which united it. This, of course, is the
idea of the 'cultural nation' which Herder had expounded
before Fichte developed it into the idea of the 'political
nation'; and in Berchet's essay there is more than a hint of the
'literary fatherland' of Italy giving birth to a 'political fatherland'. The revolutionary implications of Italian romanticism
are generally more evident in Berchet's essay than in the other
manifesti, but at the same time, his language is more elevated,
and his appeal to the Christian conscience more direct. What
is wrong with classicism, he insists, is that its morality is
pagan. The world of classical antiquity is a bad model because
its people worshipped false gods. Romanticism, by contrast,
is Christian because it springs from a faith in a redeeming
Lord, in eternal life and the fear of damnation. It expresses the
'civilization of the living century' and is 'the mirror of what
moves the spirit with the greatest intensity'.

In later years Berchet came to think that he had perhaps
exaggerated the political elements in art, and 'sacrificed the
duties of the poet to the duties of the citizen'; but if this is a
fault, it is one for which most Italian Romantics would have
to reproach themselves. Nicolini, for example, defined romanticism as 'liberalism in art and politics' and De Cristoforis
spoke of the purpose of poetry as forwarding the 'essential
goal of liberal institutions, inspiring respect for religion, love
of one's country and admiration for all that is great and
illustrious'. These words appeared in *Il Conciliatore*, the journal of Italian romanticism, shortly before it was closed down
by the Austrian authorities in 1819.

Literary criticism had, however, by that time achieved its
purpose. Italian poetry had been freed from the constraints of
classicism. In 1818 a new voice was heard, as fresh as that of
Keats, as patriotic as Foscolo: that of Giacomo Leopardi. The
sickly, hunchbacked son of an impoverished noble family in
the Marches, Leopardi was twenty when he thrilled the Italian

public with two *canzoni* on national themes: the first of these
is '*All' Italia*', which laments the afflictions of Italy under
Napoleonic rule and foresees a future rising of the nation in
arms; the second is '*Sopra il monumento di Dante*', which sum-
mons Italians to reflect on the glorious dead of the past and
make themselves worthy of their patrimony. In these early
years, Leopardi wrote several poems inspired by Rousseau's
teaching about the divinity of nature and the natural innocence of man, but in the poems of his later years – as a
result perhaps of his unhappy experience of life as an un-
wanted cripple – he no longer asserts the goodness but the
cruelty of nature which implants in man desires it prevents
him from satisfying. A number of Leopardi's lyrics dwell on
the subject of unrequited love. '*Consalvo*' is about a young
poet who dies happily because his dying prompts his beloved
Elvira to take pity on him and kiss him. In his '*Storia del genere
umano*' Leopardi declares that love is an illusion, but a beautiful illusion because it confers richness on the lives of those
few chosen souls who can feel it. Leopardi's later writings no
longer express hope for happiness or even for the future of
freedom in Italy, and his very last poem, '*La ginestra*', written
as he lay dying in Naples at the age of thirty-nine, seems to
anticipate the bitter nihilism of Nietzsche:

> Nature has no more heart
> Or care for human seed than for the ants.

Lines of this kind shocked certain devout admirers of Leopardi's poetry, including the British Liberal statesman William Ewart Gladstone, who wrote one of the first English
appreciations of Leopardi, praising the lyrical qualities but
deploring what he called 'the absence of that Gospel revelation, without which even while we feel the poet to be an
enchanter, we cannot accept and trust him as a guide'. This
was not, however, the response which Leopardi evoked in his
Italian readers. They were able to sense the idealism behind

his disillusionment. The critic Francesco De Sanctis, who as a boy had met Leopardi in Naples, wrote:

> Leopardi produces an effect opposite to the one he proposes. He does not believe in progress but he makes you yearn for it. He does not believe in freedom and he makes you love it . . . He is a sceptic and he makes you a believer. He has the lowest opinion of humanity, while his lofty, pure and gentle spirit honours and ennobles it.

If Leopardi is remembered today as the finest poet of Italian romanticism, its greatest prose writer is undoubtedly Alessandro Manzoni, who made with one single book – his novel *I promessi sposi* – a monumental contribution to the *Risorgimento*. Like the literary critics of *Il Conciliatore*, Manzoni was Milanese, and although he did not write for their journal, he was on friendly terms with them and in close sympathy with their thinking; his creative writing embodied all the principles they laid down as theory; he was wholly committed to the ideal of art as the true voice of feeling, to the Catholic tradition in faith and morals, and to liberal, even republican aims in politics.

Manzoni came from a milieu that might have been thought to make him antagonistic to romanticism: that of the hedonist and rationalist Enlightenment. His maternal grandfather was the illustrious progressive jurist Beccaria; and when his mother deserted his father – his putative father, that is, for Manzoni is said by his biographers to have been the natural son of Giovanni Verri – to live in France with a very rich lover, Carlo Imbonati, she became the neighbour and intimate friend of the widows Condorcet and Helvétius, in whose *salons* Manzoni met in his youth the intellectuals who were keeping alive in the Napoleonic empire the ideas of the *Encyclopédistes*: Cabanis, Maine de Biran, Destutt de Tracy, Fauriel.

At the time, he seems to have shared their rationalism and scepticism, but at the age of twenty-three, soon after his marriage to a Swiss Protestant named Henrietta Blondel, Manzoni experienced a religious illumination, and converted to Catholicism (as did his wife) under the influence of Monsignor Tosi, an exponent of the puritanical, evangelical form of Catholicism known as Jansenism. Henceforth, Manzoni led a life of studious piety, giving certain hours of the day to writing and as many to prayers and devotions. Under the instruction of Monsignor Tosi, he threw into a bonfire seventeen volumes of the finely-bound edition of the *Works* of Voltaire that he had brought from France to his home in Lombardy.

That house was one his mother had contrived to inherit, together with another in Milan, on the death of her lover, an estate more considerable than the modest property of the Manzoni family near Lecco. By continuing to live under his mother's roof, Manzoni was able to enjoy a feudal kind of life, untroubled by material needs or bourgeois social duties. He discouraged people from addressing him as 'Conte', although the Manzonis had as good a claim to that title as most in Lombardy who used it; but it was noticed that while he kept company for the most part with middle-class writers and intellectuals, it was to persons of nobility alone that he spoke with the familiar *'tu'*. Manzoni remained, however, a staunch republican. He refused all offers of honours and decorations from the Austrians, and even to receive a Hapsburg prince who called at his house. It was with considerable reluctance that he accepted, on the unification of Italy under the Savoyard monarchy in 1861, an appointment as Senator. By that time, however, he had resigned himself to the fact that he had become almost an institution, and that it was his duty to assume some public office.

Manzoni's earliest poems, *Inni sacri*, were on religious themes, and his first notable prose writings, the *Osservazioni* of 1819, set out to defend the Church against Sismondi's argument, in his history of the Italian republics, that Catholicism was responsible for the corruption of Italian civic life in the Middle Ages. But it was with a verse drama on a secular historical subject – *Il conte di Carmagnola* – that Manzoni made his name in 1820. In a letter to his French friend Fauriel he explained that he had written *Carmagnola* after making a thorough study of Shakespeare, and that he had been emboldened by that example to discard the rules of the unities and most of the other Aristotelian principles of drama. In a published preface to the play Manzoni defended his adhesion to what was by this time freely spoken of in Italy as *romantismo*. The play is in fact rather less like anything by Shakespeare himself than it is like Goethe's 'Shakespearean' *Götz von Berlichingen*, in both content and style. Goethe, indeed, was one of the first and most enthusiastic admirers of Manzoni's play, and he continued to shower encouragement and praise on the author for the rest of his life.

Carmagnola is about a condottiere of plebeian origins who serves bravely and well under the Visconti of Milan, but after being shabbily treated by his patron, transfers his services to the Venetians and leads their armies to victory against the Milanese. His reward is to be accused of treason by the Venetian Doge and Senate, condemned to death and executed. The argument of the play proved to be highly controversial. Carmagnola was regarded by most Milanese historians as a turncoat who deserved his fate: Manzoni presented him as the innocent victim of political intrigue, a man of courage in noble conflict with the petty ambitions of Italy's *quattrocento* leaders. The implication is that Italy's divisions are to be seen as the consequence of corruption in government and that one noble individual might serve as a vessel for regeneration.

A secondary theme of *Carmagnola* is Manzoni's suggestion that history is to be understood as a divine order, towards which short-term judgement must give way to acceptance of the higher wisdom of Providence. The most intensely moving part of the play is the last act, in which the hero explains his conception of a Christian life and his acceptance of a Christian death. *Carmagnola*, however, is a play to be read. Unlike Goethe, Manzoni had no sense of the stage, no talent for providing material for actors to act. When *Carmagnola* was performed at Florence, it was a total failure.

Manzoni, still aspiring to be a dramatist, wrote another play *Adelchi*, which is often spoken of as his *Hamlet*, if only because the title is the name of the central character, a prince who broods on the injustice of the world. But Manzoni's hero is not, like Hamlet, a man tormented by indecision; he is presented as a man upheld by Christian faith, 'seeing life on earth as a state of trial and preparation for the life to come', as Manzoni explained it in his notes on the play. Furthermore, *Adelchi* was not designed to be a play primarily about Adelchi. It was intended to recount the history of the conquest of Northern Italy by the barbarian Longobards, the intervention of the Franks at the behest of the Pope, and the failure of that policy to alleviate the sufferings of the indigenous people. In a letter to Fauriel, Manzoni noted that 'one scarcely finds a mention of the Italian people in the histories of Lombardy', and in a preface to the printed version of *Adelchi* he again criticizes historians for recording only the deeds of great men while ignoring the experience of the 'immense multitude of ordinary men and women who live on their own native piece of earth without leaving a trace in history'. Manzoni's play was meant to give voice to the feelings of those ordinary people, and also to denounce the view, established in historians' textbooks, that the Longobard rule over those ordinary people had been 'paternal' – a purpose which was equally a denunciation of the claim that current Austrian rule in Lombardy was 'benevolent'.

Yet for all his concern for 'the people', Manzoni was not able, like Michelet to rid himself of fascination with the individual. Jansenism may have taught him to hate the self, but he never ceased to be enthralled by the unique personalities of others, by heroes, flawed heroes and anti-heroes, by all those whom Diderot called '*les originaux*'. Even Napoleon came to be included in this category. Although Manzoni attacked him as a tyrant in *Adelchi* in the thin disguise of 'Charlemagne', he wrote, on Napoleon's death in 1821 an ode to the Emperor's memory entitled *Il cinque maggio*. 'Was his glory true?' the poet asks, and he can hardly be said to answer in the negative. The ode first depicts Napoleon as the triumphant soldier – a man whom God 'has chosen to mark with His creative spirit'; it goes on to show him defeated, a melancholy prisoner of St Helena, yet also a philosopher, reflecting on the ephemeral nature of all things human. 'Deprived of a soul so great', the poet cries, 'the earth lies stricken and astonished.'

Goethe, again, greeted the ode with the warmest praise, and promptly set about translating it into German. It was admired everywhere as a model of romantic verse. It also had an effect which the poet had not intended: it contributed, as did so much else in romantic literature in the 1820s, to a cult of Napoleon throughout the western world. As life became more drab in the smoky cities of the industrial revolution, amid the frock coats and top hats of the bourgeois ascendancy, the colourful figure of the fallen Emperor acquired a glamour which none of the restored rulers could match, even in the eyes of the Italians who had lately suffered under Napoleon's oppression.

Manzoni's two plays had been concerned in turn with what he saw as the two great obstacles to Italian freedom: disunity in *Carmagnola*; alien rule in *Adelchi*. In his eyes the disunity was in some ways the greater problem, and certainly a greater problem for Italy than it was for Germany. At least the Germans, for all the multiplicity of petty principalities into which their country was divided, spoke one language; Germany, as Herder had expressed it, was a 'cultural nation'. Italy, Manzoni realized, was not yet one. Italians spoke a variety of different dialects; their various regions and localities had each

a large measure of cultural singularity as well as each its own
political, economic and social history. In this situation, Manzoni argued that Italian artists had a crucial contribution to
make to the liberation of Italy by providing it with the
common national identity which it lacked, and Italian writers
the particular duty of promoting a standard Italian language
which could seal the Italian people together in the bond of a
common tongue.

To succeed in this enterprise, Manzoni knew he would have
to reach a vast public. The enormous success of Sir Walter
Scott gave him an idea of how it might be done. After writing
the two historical plays which no theatre would stage, he
decided to write a historical novel like one of Scott's in the
hope of reaching a universal audience. The project plunged
him into many months of research – not only into history,
but also into language, for he was determined that this novel
should offer a model of pure Italian prose, a standard for
common acceptance throughout Italy. He had read many
more French books than he had Italian, and learned from
them that a prose writer's ideal should be to incorporate in
the written language the simplicity and euphony of the
spoken word. This meant the banishment of 'literary Italian'
with all its pomp and rhetoric. It also meant the search for a
systematic framework of grammar, syntax and vocabulary,
and it was in pursuit of this goal that Manzoni went from
Lombardy to Tuscany, where the descendants of Machiavelli
and Dante had maintained what seemed to him the closest to
perfection in the Italian language.

Manzoni had already drafted in Milan his Walter Scott-like
novel, and in Florence he set about revising it to incorporate
Tuscan usages and forms. He began by changing the title
from *Gli sposi promessi* to the more euphonious *I promessi sposi*
and he went on to make modifications of a more substantial
kind, correcting and polishing the style over and over again,
in months, even years of fastidious effort. The result is a book

which is a joy to read, even for its language alone. *I promessi sposi* has been described as 'a Christian *Candide*'; and clearly, despite Monsignor Tosi's having made Manzoni burn his Voltaire volumes, he could not destroy Manzoni's memory of how those books were written: and *I promessi sposi* reproduces in Italian the lucidity, elegance and wit of Voltaire's French.

Manzoni was hardly less diligent in the attention he gave to historical detail. The novel is about the adventures in seventeenth-century Lombardy of two young peasants, who try to get married but are constantly thwarted by ill luck and the machinations of the wicked. Prolonged research informed Manzoni's descriptions of what life was like at the time of Spanish rule in Italy: the wars, lawsuits, plagues, famines and other notable events are recorded with scrupulous attention to the available evidence, as are the details of everyday life in the various social milieux in which Manzoni's characters move. Some of these characters are real people: Cardinal Borromeo, for example, the Chancellor Ferrer, and Virginia de Leyva, the so-called 'Nun of Monza', whose love affair with a Spanish *bravo* Manzoni introduced into the story, to the horror of Monsignor Tosi. Yet it is the imaginary characters who seem the most real, thanks to the psychological insight of the novelist and his creative genius. Don Abbondio, for instance, the pusillanimous priest who dares not marry the little peasant sweethearts, is surely an immortal figure in the mind of anyone who has read *I promessi sposi*; and even the very minor figures, such as the crooked lawyer, Dr Azzeccagarbugli, are as three-dimensional as any character in Molière.

The novel was an instant and universal success when it was published in 1827. Goethe, once more, greeted it eagerly: 'Everything which is of the poet's soul, everything which is of the poet's heart is perfect . . . One passes continuously from tenderness to admiration'. Lamartine said the novel was 'one of the three or four books I have read with the most enchantment in my whole life'. In Italy, it was devoured by readers of every class. It was something more than a mere book; it became the object of a cult, a sacred text of the patriotic movement, a vital force in the *Risorgimento*.

Between 1827 and 1840, Manzoni continued to bring out revised and improved versions of *I promessi sposi*. He realized that it was his masterpiece, and he had no expectation of producing anything to equal it, although he lived to be eighty-eight. His personal life was never easy. His formidable mother loomed over him at home until her death in 1841; his first wife had been constantly ill up to her death in 1833; five of his daughters all died young, and those who lived were invalids; his sons were spendthrifts and drunkards. His second wife was a neurotic valetudinarian, who died twelve years before he did. If anyone needed the consolations of religion, Manzoni needed them amid the sorrows of a house he seldom left. And yet with a single beautifully written, romantic novel this sombre Jansenist inspired the whole of Italy with pride and hope.

If Manzoni's efforts were directed to the consolidation of Italy as a cultural nation, those of his contemporary Giuseppe Mazzini were directing its development as a political nation; in his approach to this purpose Mazzini was no less romantic than Manzoni. He, too, was influenced by Jansenism, having been educated by Jansenist priests at school; their combination of moral inflexibility with piety shaped his character, so that when he turned from literature to politics, Mazzini resisted all the temptations to compromise and accommodation which politics commonly entails, to remain the pure uncorrupted and often ineffective idealist.

He began as a writer, an essayist of the romantic school, publishing work on such subjects as Dante's *amor patrio*, on Providence as an element in drama and on the philosophy of music. When he turned to more political themes, the religious element was no less evident. The emphasis is on sacrifice rather than success and on the duties rather than the rights of man. Mazzini spoke of his decision to turn aside from literary activity to commit himself to the cause of Italian nationalism as the 'call to an apostolate'. It was a call which led him to plunge himself into intense and often dangerous activity as the organizer of groups dedicated to the creation of a free and united Italy. The youth movement *Giovane Italia* was the best known of these, but there were other more secret organizations, whose activities obliged Mazzini to spend much of his life in exile.

His Rousseauesque vision was for the Italian people to take the sovereignty of their nation into their own hands. What he did not want was for Italy to be unified from above by one of its regional princes extending his dominion over the whole of the peninsula: he had hoped never to see what did eventually happen in 1861, when the Savoyard King of Sardinia, with French support, made himself King of Italy, to the satisfaction of most Italian nationalists including Alessandro Manzoni. Mazzini did not shrink from violence. He had a hand in several provincial risings which were soon suppressed and which would never have been launched by a more practical, less visionary, political intelligence. Mazzini himself was driven out of France and of Switzerland as a dangerous insurrectionist, then settled in England where he was greatly admired by liberals and Romantics alike. Thomas Carlyle called him 'a man of genius and virtue' and a 'hero'. Nationalists in Poland and Hungary found inspiration in his person and his writings. Garibaldi took his irregular army into battle on Sicilian and Italian soil with the aim of making Mazzini's dream come true.

The last years of Mazzini's life were perhaps the unhappiest, after the pre-emptive union of Italy by the princes and politicians as a kingdom had thwarted its union by the people as a republic; he returned to Italy, but only to be forced to live under a false name and in hiding, a fugitive in his own country until his death at Pisa in 1872. Carlyle's 'hero' thus ended as another of romanticism's martyrs.

Italian music, we have noticed, played a central role in the formation of romantic taste, and in Rousseau's early argument for romantic aesthetics. Pergolesi provided the model of composition Rousseau invoked in criticizing the rationalist principles of Rameau and in propelling European music towards those forms developed by Gluck and Mozart. After the French Revolution, the romantic elements in Pergolesi were reinvigorated in Italy by Gioacchino Rossini, who was known to his fellow students as 'the little German' – *Il Tedeschino* – precisely because of his devotion to Mozart and Gluck.

Rossini earned fame at an early age by composing operas for the Italian stage: *L'Italiana in Algeri* in 1813, *Il Turco in Italia* in 1814. When he moved to Paris as Director of the Théâtre Italien he composed French operas for the French stage: *Le Comte Ory* (1828) and *Guillaume Tell* (1829). Rossini was hardly an Italian nationalist; the young *Tedeschino* of the conservatory became in later years the eager francophile living in France up to the time of his death. If there is a political message in his operas it is the message of freedom for everyone: a song for the freedom of the Swiss in *Guillaume Tell*, for example, being easily taken in 1829 in Paris as a song for freedom of the French from what was felt to be the tyranny of Charles X.

It was left to Rossini's successor as the leading Italian operatic composer, Giuseppe Verdi, to produce a music that was not simply national, but nationalist. Composing for La Scala in Milan, Verdi had to work under the close eye of the Austrian censors so that he had to express patriotic sentiments in devious ways. His first really successful opera *Nabucco* was given a biblical setting and the aria '*O mia patria*' put into the mouths of Hebrews yearning for their homeland. His public promptly took it up to sing with another *patria* in mind. Other Verdi operas, *I Lombardi*, for example, set in the time of the crusades, and *Macbeth*, set in Scotland, also introduce disguised patriotic songs. In *Attila*, Italy is actually named, and the aria *'Resti l'Italia a me'* repeatedly aroused the wildest enthusiasm whenever it was sung in Italian opera houses. It was not simply that Verdi's songs were composed to patriotic words: he provided music which lifted the hearts of the listeners, introducing sounds which were unknown in eighteenth-century opera, such as the voice of the heroic tenor, to which Verdi gave a stirring eloquence and power.

Opera as an art form had long been popular in Italy to an extent unmatched elsewhere. It was also an art form with a particular attraction to the romantic spirit. The Enlightenment, with its cosmopolitan philosophy, favoured wordless orchestral music because it needs no translation and commands an international audience. Romanticism preferred opera because opera is sung, a song is poetry, poetry is language and language is what binds people together as a nation. In Verdi the fusion of romanticism and nationalism is perfected and music becomes inseparable from ideology.

6

Spanish Romanticism

The Spanish poets of nineteenth-century romanticism — Espronceda, for example, or Rivas or José Zorrilla — never enjoyed the international renown of Byron, Chateaubriand, Manzoni or the German poets. On the other hand, Spain played a dominant role in the pre-history of romantic literature; Spain was its birthplace. When the Romantics of the eighteenth and nineteenth centuries spoke of recovering the spirit of the troubadours in whose poetry of courtly love they detected something which prefigured their own work, they had in mind medieval Provence, and the Provençal language which the troubadours employed. That Provençal poetry, however, was part of a cultural movement which originated in Moorish Spain, and emerged out of the highly civilized society which the Islamic — mainly Berber — conquerors instituted in the south of the Iberian peninsula and sustained for several hundred years.

It is, in a way, ironical that the Moors, who transmitted to Christian Europe the Aristotelian philosophy of ancient Greece, on which both scholastic rationalism and neo-classical aesthetics were based, should also have provided Europe with the earliest models from which later romantic literature derived, but the links can be established on the textual evidence. Herder and other theorists of romanticism liked to believe that European lyric poetry had popular, demotic roots in the simple songs of rustic Germanic communities. In fact, the poems of the troubadours have been shown to derive from the lyrics of educated poets attached to the courts of Moorish Spain, where Arabic culture was joined by Hebrew culture to produce a literature that was far in advance of anything that existed in Christian Europe. The several small Christian kingdoms which shared the Iberian peninsula with the Moorish occupants were naturally affected by the achievements of their neighbours, notwithstanding the fact that they were sporadically at war with them. Spanish poetry written in Moorish Spain passed through these kingdoms to Provence, whose language – the language of the troubadours – was also spoken in Catalonia.

Of course, it may be that the Moorish poets themselves found some inspiration for their work in popular song, but they were professional poets employed by princely patrons, educated writers who gave their verses a formal structure and wove them around lofty ideas of which the most notable from the point of view of the troubadours and later Romantics, was that of courtly love, about which there is nothing rustic or folkloric. An early Moorish exposition of the idea of courtly love is to be found in *The Book of the Flower* by Ibn Dawud (868–910) where the author argues that love must not be allowed sexual gratification, but rather prolonged by the denial of detumescence so that it becomes an exquisite voluptuous agony. Similar thoughts are expressed in verse by Ibn Hazam and Al Mu'tamid, who both combine spirituality with a greater measure of sensuality than the Christian Spaniards who succeeded them. Those successors were no less superior persons writing for cultured readers. Al Mu'tamid was a prince of Seville; and among the best early poets of Christian Spain were King Dinis of Portugal and King Alfonso of Castille.

Many of the earliest Spanish love poems were, however, written from a woman's perspective. What came to be known as *cantigas de amigo* express, like the earlier *kharjas*, a girl's heart-stirrings and her yearning for an absent lover. If the first recorded poetry in the Spanish language is thus a feminine poetry, it may be due to the fact that Spanish in Moorish Spain was the domestic language, spoken by the indigenous wives of the Moorish occupants, who used Arabic for official and public purposes. The masculine counterpart of the *cantigas de amigo* were the *cantigas de amor*, and it is in these that we find the best early expression of the idea of courtly love.

It is a similar concept to that of the Provençal troubadours, but not quite the same. Nor should we expect it to be, for Provence was significantly different from Christian Spain. Provence, like the rest of France, was feudal where Spain was royal, whether under Moorish princes in the south or under kings in Aragon, Navarre, Castile, León, Galicia and Portugal. Provence, when the troubadours appeared on the scene towards the year 1100 AD, had produced a brilliant, sophisticated society in which freedom of thought and action alternated with arrogant assertions of baronial despotism. Spain, constantly at war with the Infidel, was more steadily authoritarian, disciplined and law-abiding, more respectful of the throne and altar. The concept of courtly love is more worldly in Provençal poetry than in the Spanish *cantigas de amor*. A twelfth-century author in France, Andreas Capellanus, attempted in his treaty *De Arte honesti amandi* to explain the Provençal understanding of courtly love. He drew a distinction between *amor purus*, which involves passion and allows a fair measure of physical contact but excludes actual consummation and, on the other hand, *amor mixtus*, which ends in sexual congress and is therefore sinful. Courtly love, said Andreas, is a form of *amor purus*. This is very much the kind of love which Rousseau experienced with Mme d'Houdetot and which he allows St-Preux and Julie to enjoy in the later chapters of *La nouvelle Héloïse*; but one has only to read a few of the Provençal poets to see that what Andreas offers is not a true account of their concept of love. For while they show little interest in married love, adulterous love is by no means always excluded. Guillaume, Comte de Poitiers, who flourished at the end of the eleventh century, and is generally considered the first of the troubadour poets, clearly authorizes sexual congress, provided only that it is secret:

> All the joy in the world is ours
> My lady, if only we two can love.

By love, the poet obviously means what Andreas calls *amor mixtus*. Later troubadour verse praises love in the same sense. But if Andreas was thus mistaken about the Provençal conception of courtly love, his analysis is doubtless true of the Spanish. His book was, in any case, for many years more highly regarded in Spain than elsewhere.

The first characteristic of courtly love in Spanish literature is that it is courtly – felt as a noble sentiment and expressed with elegance; and although physical desire is a part of it, that physical desire is not simply denied satisfaction, but transformed into a metaphysical, sometimes even a religious feeling. Whether sincerely or not, the suitor humbles himself before his lady, declares himself unworthy of her, yet also claims that if she returns his love he will attain virtue; he promises obedience to her wishes and caprices and begs her to command him as mistress. In the *cantigas de amor*, this courtly love is love at a distance and sometimes it is not even requited; besides, the frustration is felt as a tragic misfortune, seldom as the kind of voluptuous agony that is expressed in both Moorish and Provençal lyrics.

Nevertheless, the Spanish poets learned from the Provençal troubadours just as the troubadours learned from them, for when the tomb of St James at Santiago di Compostella became a place of pilgrimage, visitors from beyond the Pyrenees brought with them to Galicia their poetry and music, prompting in that kingdom a flowering of pastoral verse in which a rather simpler form of love than courtly love is celebrated. The Galician *pastourelle* tells of the loves of shepherds and shepherdesses in a spirit we should today think of 'Rousseauesque'; for it is the kind of love depicted in Rousseau's *Le Devin du village*, the love of little people who live close to nature and are uncorrupted by urbanized society. In the Galician *pastourelle*, the lovers are usually denied the gratification they are allowed in French pastorals; as in the *cantigas de amor* caresses are allowed, but actual sexual congress is denied.

The popularity of the *pastourelle* in Galicia has been plausibly ascribed to the fact that it was the custom in that kingdom for upper-class families to send their children to the country villages not only to be wet-nursed, but to be brought up to adolescence, so that seigneurial Galician youth must have felt the first stirrings of the heart in a milieu of shepherdesses and dairymaids, far removed from the world of palaces and castles where courtly poetry was written and recited. Castilian poets were less charmed by rustic simplicity; and although the pastoral has its place in later romantic literature in other countries, it does not figure in the Romantic Movement of nineteenth-century Spain.

When the latter-day Romantics spoke of reviving the spirit of the troubadours, they usually coupled that plea with an evocation of 'the age of chivalry', conceived as embodying the highest achievements of medieval Christian culture. It was in Spain that chivalry was most assiduously cultivated. Precisely because Spain was an almost permanent battleground for war between Christians and Moslems, many foreign knights rode their mounts to the peninsular to help the Spanish Christians resist the Infidel and often also to engage in skirmishes among themselves. It was in this context that codes of chivalry – which were originally designed to regulate the conduct of Christian combatants in war – were developed; and the literary expression of those codes emerged as *libros de caballe-ria* or 'books of chivalry'. Participation in the Crusades extended the activity of knights elsewhere and enlarged the scope of chivalry as a school of honour, gallantry and courtesy for noblemen and gentlemen throughout Christendom, but Spain remained the focal point and the most fertile breeding ground of the literature of chivalry.

Even before the age of chivalry, Spain produced works of heroic poetry which survived to stir the romantic imagination of later generations. Already in the middle of the twelfth century, there appeared a remarkable work written in Castilian by a Mozarabic author and known as the *Poema de mio Cid*, 'Cid' being a derivative of the Arabic *'sidi'* or 'lord'. It tells of the exploits of a Castilian condottiere, Rodrigo Diaz, who wins fame as a leader of men in many wars. Diaz is a social upstart, but his military triumphs win him the favour of the King of Castile, who rewards him by designating princely bridegrooms for his two daughters. However, both bridegrooms resent a match they consider beneath them, and first abuse, then abandon their wives. The Cid thereupon demands the right to avenge his honour in single combat, and the story ends with the princes defeated and the daughters married into the royal houses of Navarre and Aragon.

Clearly what appealed to the Romantics in this story was the idea of a humble soldier rising, like Napoleon, to be the equal of kings. Although *El Cid* was adapted by Corneille in the seventeenth century into a classical conflict between love and honour, in the original *poema*, the hero is no paragon of moral scruples, but a flawed hero, animated more often by ambition than by duty, far from constant in his loyalties, and less a forerunner of Corneille's *Cid* than of Goethe's *Götz von Berlichingen* or Manzoni's *Conte di Carmagnola*.

The first real 'book of chivalry' appeared about the year 1300 with the title *El Caballero Zifar*. It relates, in the form of prose fiction, the career of the knight Zifar, as he rises in the course of many adventures from obscure origins to be a king. Unlike El Cid, Zifar succeeds solely by the exercise of virtue, piety and courage. Moreover, where the adventures of El Cid in the *poema* are such as could have happened, and in the light of historical research seem mostly to have actually happened, those of Zifar are extraordinary, incredible, fabulous. This latter is also true of most *libros de caballeria*; imagination runs riot in them: giants and dragons are commonplace; whole armies are routed by one hero's sword; lost children are washed ashore alive on the tides; vice is always punished and virtue most lavishly rewarded.

The first of these novels to be actually printed was *Tirant lo Blanch*, a Catalan work, published in 1490, and soon translated into Spanish, French and other languages. It was still being read in the France of the Enlightenment, admired by Rousseau and his circle at Montmorency, which included at that time Diderot. It is worth considering what recommended it to the first two theorists of modern romanticism. The plot is as improbable as any. In the first part, an English earl, after two short weeks of married bliss, is afflicted by remorse for his sins and leaves home to fight in turn a Saracen giant and an African giant, then retires to lead a hermit's life, where he is visited by Tirant lo Blanch, a French squire, who is inspired by his conversations with the earl to undertake a series of prodigious deeds, defeating kings and dukes in tournaments, relieving the siege of Rhodes by the Sultan of Cairo, winning the imperial crown of Greece and the hand of a princess in marriage, only to die in the end of a commonplace sickness. *Tirant lo Blanch*, however, is a book which rises above the improbability of the events it narrates. It is singularly realistic in its depiction of the inwardness of its characters: it is infused with a sentimental idealism and almost lyrical evocation of an unseen world.

The next great *libro de caballeria*, published in Castilian in 1508, is *Amadis de Gaula*, which endures, despite the fabulous events it records, as a genuine work of imagination, as distinct from what Coleridge called mere fancy. Amadis, in this tale, is the natural son of a king of Wales, put to sea by his mother as an infant in an ark, rescued by a Scottish knight and introduced to the court of Scotland where he falls in love with a royal princess. To justify his claim to the princess's hand, Amadis assumes the profession of arms and proves himself in many tournaments and battles, the best knight in the world, the noblest, bravest, most courteous and magnanimous, and the most steadfast in his loyalty to his lady and his king. Love – pure love – is shown to be the motivating force of his noble and virtuous accomplishments.

Few of the numerous stories of chivalry which were written after *Amadis* achieved the same distinction, and as a genre they seem increasingly to lose touch with real life at every point. They did, however, generate, as a kind of reaction, the picaresque novel of which the central character was not a chivalrous knight doing brave deeds but a clever *picaro*, or rogue, who has less edifying, but no less enthralling adventures as he travels around the world, living on his wits. This form of fiction, which has enjoyed a fairly continuous history in European literature, may be said to date from *La Vida de Lazarillo de Tormes*, first published in 1554. It introduces that intriguing figure, the 'anti-hero', who was to play such a central role in the romantic novel of the future. When Rousseau's *Confessions* was first published in 1782, several critics declared that it was more of a picaresque novel than an autobiography, and one can understand why. If Rousseau's novel *La nouvelle Héloïse* can trace its ancestry to the *cantigas de amor*, as a tragedy of frustrated love, in the telling of his own early experience of life, wandering around Savoy and Piedmont and France, taking on odd jobs as a footman, a secretary, or a music teacher, falling in with thieves and mountebanks, seduced by older women, inventing all sorts of tricks to provide the next meal, we see a perfect reflection of that kind of novel which was first invented in sixteenth-century Spain. The truth of the matter seems to be that the best of the Spanish picaresque novels were themselves really autobiographies in disguise; in writing about the adventures of young rogues, those authors, no less than Rousseau in the eighteenth century, were writing about themselves.

The greatest of all Spanish novels, *Don Quixote* by Cervantes, is both a kind of picaresque novel and a book of chivalry, despite its being declared by the author to be 'an attack on all books of chivalry'. For although its hero is said to be mad in his devotion to chivalry, his is an attractive, even an inspiring madness; and the sanity of the world in which he looks such a foolish figure, a charmless sanity.

It may well be that *Don Quixote* changed its character as the author wrote it. The Don is introduced as a simple-minded country gentleman who puts on a suit of armour and mounts a broken-down hack he calls Rozinante and appoints as his squire an illiterate but shrewd peasant Sancho Panza. He chooses a village girl as his Lady Dulcinea and dedicates himself to her service. The ordinary people he meets he imagines to be giants, warriors or damsels in distress and, in a famous scene, he sees the sails of a windmill as armed adversaries, and tilts his lance at them. All his efforts to win chivalric honour lead him and his squire into ever more unfortunate and comical predicaments. But somehow amidst all the absurdities, the Don vindicates the nobility of his imagination; and his conversations with his squire provide a marvellous dialogue between Christian idealism and worldly wisdom. What begins as a satire ends up as a richly philosophical novel.

In the annals of romantic literary criticism, the name of Cervantes comes second only to that of Shakespeare. The novel jogs along in fits and starts like the Don on his Rozinante and, mixing tragedy and comedy, breaks most of the rules of classical literary taste; but it is a triumph, and like all really great books, has attracted readers in almost every language and has continued to be read uninterruptedly by successive generations since it was first published in 1605.

When a school of neo-classical criticism developed – belatedly – in Spain in the eighteenth century, Cervantes was something of an embarrassment to its members. He was too big a name to dismiss; but neither could they approve of his work. They chose simply to treat it as a gigantic piece of allegory. Blas Antonio Nasarre argued in a published essay that Cervantes should be read as seeking to expose the defects and extravagances of Spanish fiction by mimicking them. This became the standard view of the Academia del Buen Gusto which was established in Madrid in 1749 with the aim of imposing the discipline of classical aesthetics on Spanish writers and artists. The most systematic exposition of the classical theory was provided by Ignacio de Luzán in his *Poética*. But that book influenced very few creative writers, and was answered with equally well-argued eloquence by a Benedictine monk, Fray Benito Jéronimo Feijóo y Montenegro, who, in his *Cartas Eruditas*, disputed the suggestion that the highest forms of human expression could be reduced to rationalistic formulae or that genius should conform to the rules laid down by critics: creative art, he insisted, must be free.

Neo-classical aesthetics did not prosper in Spain; it went too much against the national character and the national literary tradition. Sismondi, who claimed that Spanish literature had 'almost always been romantic' might better have said 'preromantic', but the remark was fair enough. We have seen that Spanish literature possessed from its beginnings in Mozarabic verse several of those characteristics that were later identified as romantic, and that it provided models for foreign authors as well as native authors of various romantic tendencies.

What is known as the Romantic Movement developed relatively late in Spain. If the neo-classical critics of the eighteenth-century did little else, they put a brake on Spanish creativity; the Napoleonic Wars and the clerical reaction which followed them produced something of a cultural vacuum, and it was only after the death of the repressive Ferdinand VII in 1833 that poetry came to life again in Spain. What came to life was romantic poetry. Romanticism being then at the height of its fashion throughout Europe, it is easy to understand that no other kind of poetry would be wanted. Romanticism promised to bring Spain once more into the swim of things, and also to restore a national tradition. Several of the leading poets were liberals, and had been in exile. Foreign poets such as Byron and Lamartine were already famous in Spain; and Spanish poets of the 1830s were naturally tempted to live up to the image of the poet that those colourful, glamorous personalities had imprinted on the public mind.

José de Espronceda came closest to satisfying the Byronic specification. He was a revolutionary, forced to leave Spain to avoid arrest. He had a tempestuous love affair with a mistress who died of consumption. He paraded his ego in a series of poems of genuine lyrical distinction, and he died at the age of thirty-four in 1842.

Angel de Saavedra, Duque de Rivas, was the Spanish Lamartine – a liberal nobleman and a soldier–poet who glorified the medieval past in *leyendas*, or narrative poems composed in a variety of metres and enriched by highly coloured descriptive passages. He also wrote a series of *Romances* – a word which in Spanish had long been used to mean 'ballads' – which resemble the *Lay of the Last Minstrel* by Sir Walter Scott. Rivas is probably best remembered for his play *Don Alvaro or The Force of Destiny*, which carried a preface by Antonio Galiano, setting out what is perhaps the best exposition of Spanish nineteenth-century romanticism. When the play was first performed in Madrid in 1835, it provoked much the same kind of public excitement as the première of Victor Hugo's *Hernani* in Paris.

The third and youngest of the new romantic poets, José Zorrilla, was the most popular with the reading public. He, too, wrote *leyendas* of considerable charm together with a number of autobiographical verses enriched by his experiences of travel in the more colourful parts of Europe and America. He achieved his greatest success with *Don Juan Tenorio*, a treatment of the Don Juan legend which is far removed from Byron's version, but not for that reason any less romantic. For Byron, as we have noted, was the archetypal romantic person without being a truly romantic poet; and whereas his *Don Juan* is realistic and wordly, Zorrilla's is idealistic and other-wordly. The church gave its blessing to *Don Juan Tenorio*, doubtless because it evokes divine love even more often than profane love, and the play has always worked well on the stage despite – or perhaps because of – certain sentimental and blatantly theatrical features of which Zorrilla became half-ashamed in later years. He lived long enough to be crowned at Granada in 1889, at the age of seventy-two, as the national poet of Spain. *Granada* was the title of a long unfinished poem in which he evoked the splendours of that province under Moorish rule, a subject which enabled him to deploy all his skills of stylization, colour, decoration and complicated rhythms to disguise his sometimes rather commonplace thoughts. Moreover, in describing the world of the Infidel, he was spared any occasion to overstress the religious sentiments. Towards the end of his life, Zorrilla produced a new version of the Cid story – *La Leyenda del Cid* – which recaptured the legendary condottiere from the clutches of neo-classical hagiography and gave him back his original romantic character of a hero fatally flawed.

Zorrilla first appeared on the Spanish literary scene at the age of nineteen reciting a eulogy at the funeral of José de Mariano Larra, who is usually remembered as a journalist, but was also an important figure in the Romantic Movement in Spain. He was about the same age as Espronceda, but while

Espronceda was in exile, Larra was publishing subversive articles under various pseudonyms in the Madrid of Ferdinand VII. These articles, which describe in bitter language life as it was lived by the philistine world of post-Napoleonic Spain, earned Larra his place in the textbooks as a *costumbrista*, or satirist of the customs of society. Among the things he attacked, with fine intelligence and wit, was neo-classical aesthetics; and among the ideas he expounded or defended in his articles were those of liberal romanticism; he had an influential platform as 'Figaro', drama critic of the leading Spanish newspaper, *La Revista Espagnola*. But Larra was also a creative writer. A year after the Spanish Romantic Movement was fully launched on the death of Ferdinand VII, his play *Macias* was performed in Madrid; it proclaimed the same kind of alliance between romanticism and patriotism that writers of the post-Napoleonic generation were establishing in Italy and Germany. Larra's play, recalling an early phase of the national culture, introduced a Gallician troubadour of the fifteenth century and unfolded the drama of his impossible love. Larra also wrote a novel – *El Doncel de Don Enrique* – which is again given a medieval setting, but which is rather more radical than most Spanish romantic writing. It is a sustained protest against the laws of marriage which keep love in chains, and against the laws of vassalage which keep men in slavery.

Larra, who wrote only prose, was no less than Espronceda the perfect embodiment of a popular image of the romantic poet; but in his case, the model was Werther not Byron. He was handsome and brave, and lived only for liberty and love. At the age of sixteen he had his first affair with a woman who turned out to be his father's mistress; at twenty, he made an unfortunate marriage, then embarked on an adulterous liaison with a woman who eventually left him. Broken-hearted by the desertion, Larra committed suicide at the age of twenty-seven.

The two writers of the Spanish Romantic Movement who are most admired today, Gustavo Adolfo Bécquer and Rosalía Castro, were less appreciated in their lifetime. Bécquer's private life was not unlike Larra's: he made the same sort of unsuitable marriage, had similar unhappy love affairs, and without even enjoying anything like Larra's literary success, died of consumption at the age of thirty-three. His most impressive works are love poems, rich in beautiful similes, as in these lines to his wife:

> You grow out of the void of my life
> As a flower grows in a desert.

There is a kind of economy, even austerity in Bécquer's verse which proved more appealing to the taste of the twentieth century than to that of his contemporaries. His *rimas* are heavy with a pessimism which is perhaps more German than Spanish; for while death is a theme from which no Spanish writer shrinks, Bécquer is unlike other Spanish writers in lingering on pain and despair with a remorseless, hopeless intensity. His prose is more exhilarating than his verse, if less original. He wrote *leyendas* with medieval settings, introducing nymphs, giants and other supernatural creatures, and also an autobiography in the form of letters, *Desde mi Celda*. None of his work appeared in book form until after his death.

Rosalía Castro was almost his exact contemporary, being born in Santiago de Compostella in 1837. As the illegitimate child of a noble family, she had a wretched childhood, escaped to Madrid at the age of nineteen, married a dwarf who abused her; then, after giving birth to five children, she died at the age of forty-eight. Her husband, however, moved in literary circles and she was able to find a publisher for her poems. Unwisely, perhaps, she chose to write her first poem in the historic language of the Spanish lyric, Galician, a language no longer fully understood by nineteenth-century Spaniards; and it was not until the appearance of a volume of poems written in Castilian entitled *En las orilla del sar* that Rosalía Castro acquired a national reputation, and a year later she was dead. All her verse is characterized by a melancholy quality which resembles that of Bécquer but no other Spanish poet; a black sadness, a pain that is felt on flayed flesh, but tempered by a sense of divine grace.

If Bécquer and Rosalía Castro are today the most admired poets of the Spanish Romantic Movement, they are in many ways the least representative. They are not the only ones to give voice to melancholy feelings: in a collection of *Cancionero y Romancero* which Augustin Durán published in 1829, he writes of the 'melancholy' which many of those poems express, but it is, he observes, a sweet melancholy, a *dulce melancolia*. The hero of López Soler's novel *Los Bandos de Castilla* of 1830 is said to have a 'melancholy mind'; but it is a 'gentle melancholy'. The melancholy of Bécquer and Rosalía Castro is neither sweet nor gentle; it is bitter and profound. It is also unmistakably real; whereas that of Espronceda, for example, seems largely theatrical, put on when a change of mood seems called for.

Spanish romanticism is for the most part conspicuously lacking in that lachrymose quality which Rousseau encouraged and in which many German Romantics rejoiced; Spanish Romantics were too proudly masculine to weep; and the one great woman poet among them, Rosalía Castro, was, like Emily Brontë in England, too fiercely passionate for tears. Ventura de la Vega, a writer of the so-called Eclectic school, declared that any melancholy elements in Spanish poetry were the consequence of French influence: melancholy, he claimed, was alien to the national character.

Nationalism was as much a feature of Spanish as it was of German and Italian romanticism, but it was nationalism of a somewhat different order. Spain had been united as a nation state since the marriage of Ferdinand and Isabella in 1469: so that the Spanish Romantics had not, like the German and

Italian Romantics in the nineteenth century, to help create a nation; rather they saw their purpose as asserting the particular national identity, the Spanishness of Spain; and this entailed a repudiation of anything considered foreign, including the kind of cosmopolitanism which was characteristic of French romanticism.

Since Spain was, as we have seen, uniquely rich in pre-romantic literature, the Romantic Movement could fairly consider itself to be a movement of revival rather than of revolt; a return to a tradition, which the cult of neo-classicism in the eighteenth century had simply interrupted. The nationalism of the Spanish Romantics amounted to little more than patriotism magnified.

The love of country is especially notable in the work of Rivas, who nearly died on the battlefield in fighting for his country. It is a feeling that often goes together with an attachment to a particular region; in Rivas's case to Andalusia; in Zorrilla's to Granada, in Rosalía Castro's to Galicia. But there is little evidence in nineteenth-century Spanish romanticism of any Rousseauesque love of the countryside. Rivas is said to have hated leaving the town, even for the purposes of hunting. References to flowers, birds and trees and other natural beauties in Spanish romantic poetry are as trivial and formal as anything in rococo verse. Such elements seem to be introduced purely for decorative purposes, even by those women poets such as Carolina Coronado and Gertrudis Gómez, who clearly had an authentic love of nature.

There was little temptation for the Spanish Romantics to develop such love of nature into a religious cult in the way that Rousseau did, for romanticism in Spain was deeply attached to the established religion. In this respect it differed notably from romanticism elsewhere. The Christianity which later Spanish Romantics cherished was not only far removed from the vague religiosity of Chateaubriand and Lamartine and the nostalgic medievalism of Wackenroder and Tieck, but also from the puritanical Jansenist Catholicism of Manzoni and Mazzini. The Christianity of the Spanish Romantics was that of the baroque counter-Reformation church, the church of the Inquisition and the Society of Jesus, an institutionalized faith, solidly rooted in ritual, ceremonial, pomp, display and, of course, discipline. The concepts of throne and altar are repeatedly evoked in the verses of Zorrilla, and Rivas always depicts both the re-conquest of the peninsula and the conquest of the New World as triumphs of the church militant no less than of the Spanish kings.

In their obedience to the church, the Spanish Romantics were less tempted than others to brood excessively on the inner life of the self. The egoism of Espronceda is an egoism of display not of introspection, an outward-looking egoism that seeks the attention of others rather than any greater knowledge of itself. Bécquer stands apart from the mainstream of Spanish romanticism partly because of the inwardness of his writing, a characteristic which his critics suggested must be due to the fact that he was more Flemish in his origins than Spanish. That literary form so favoured by Romantics elsewhere – the *roman de l'individu* – had few exponents in Spain – Estanislao de Cosca Vayo's *Voyleano*, a novel in epistolary form, comes close to being one, but the author protested that it should not be read as yet another *Werther*.

If the Spanish Romantics had looked to any foreign theorist to expound their aesthetics, they would have looked to Diderot. For like Diderot, they loved things exotic, the bad as well as the good, the grotesque as much as the comely, anything that was different and original. They had strong stomachs. Zorrilla's *Don Juan Tenorio* ends with the hero, over a meal of fire and ashes, watching the dead come back to dig his grave and sing dirges around his bier. In Rivas's *Moro Expósito*, we see the father grasp the severed head of his youngest son and kiss its cheek. Blood flows copiously throughout the verses of both these authors. Espronceda's narrative poems are peopled with criminals, bandits, pirates cast in heroic roles, together with slaves, orphans and other unfortunates to serve as objects of pity.

The central ideal of the Spanish Romantics was also one they shared with Diderot: liberty. Rivas once said 'I made no attempt to give lessons to the world or to improve society'. But of course he did, and they all did, not least Rivas and his fellow exiles who returned to Spain in 1833. Their writings were all dedicated to the cause of freedom. If some of the Romantics moved to the Right with the unfolding of events that was perhaps because they considered freedom best served by liberal policies at one stage in history and by conservative policies at another; it was not simply the case that those who lived long enough turned reactionary with age.

In any case, if there were few left-wing voices after 1848 among the leading literary figures, romanticism exercised a powerful influence over radical thought in Spain. Spanish socialist organizations, syndicalists and other working-class groups were stirred by the romantic ideal of liberty to rally to the anarchist policies of Proudhon and Bakunin more readily than to the communist programme of Marx to which similar movements in the north of Europe were attracted.

The romantic gospel of liberty also gave rise to other ideological developments which the romantic poets of the 1830s would have deplored, including the separatist movements in Catalonia and the Basque province that threatened the unity of the Spanish state which those poets prized so highly. In the case of Catalonia, in particular, the emergence of separatism can be dated from the literary *Renaixensa* of the 1860s, when the revival under romantic auspices of the medieval poetry festivals or *Jocs Florals* prompted the recovery of Catalan – the forgotten language of *Tirant lo Blanch* – as the spoken language of the educated classes, and with it the widespread opinion – and feeling – that Catalonia, rather than Spain, was the nation to which the inhabitants belonged.

7

Late Romanticism

The experience of Spain demonstrates that romanticism has a longer history than that of the Romantic Movement. It also reminds us that the word 'romanticism' can have more than one meaning. On the one hand, it may be used in a narrow and fairly specific way to refer to what has been the main subject of this book, and for which the word 'romantic' was first introduced into European languages: the current of cultural and intellectual forces which prevailed after the decline of the Age of Reason and was in part a reaction against the values of that age. This is the romanticism of Rousseau and his successors in the Romantic Movement. On the other hand, the word 'romanticism' may be used in a broader sense to designate a certain character or spirit in art which can be contrasted with the classical by reason of its freedom from formalities and conventions, its pursuit of the truths of feeling and imagination, its inwardness and subjectivity. Since art of this kind can be traced back at least as far as early medieval times, there is nothing to be gained by stipulating a precise definition of the romantic which would confine it to modernity.

Hegel, in his writings on aesthetics, denies *die romantische Schule* an exclusive right to the title of romantic. He speaks of the romantic as one of three categories of art, the third of the three. Hegel's first is symbolic art, in which the created object or image refers to something beyond itself without embodying or transforming it. Symbolic art derives its splendour – for it may be sublime as well as beautiful – from that which it symbolizes, divinity, for example, or royalty or some other metaphysical or moral power. Hegel's second category is that of the classical, art which embodies its ideal in itself. A classical work of art, as Hegel puts it, is complete; it does not symbolize its subjects, it incorporates them: 'in a Greek statue of Apollo, Apollo is present in the stone'. Romantic art, by contrast, is an art which cannot endure the constraining imperatives of harmony and balance and measure imposed by the classical mode. Hegel suggests that romantic art arises from the Christian conception of man as an individual, as a unique being, free and immaterial, created in the image of God but alienated from him. Romantic art derives from such restless, searching spirits the testimony of personal vision and 'weaves the inner life of beauty into the contingency of external form'.

In his theory of aesthetics, Hegel passes rather rapidly from the conceptual to the historical dimension, placing symbolic art in the age of pharaonic Egypt and remote antiquity, classical art in that of ancient Greece and Rome, and romantic art in the Christian centuries. Any such periodization must be controversial, but Hegel is surely correct in pointing to Christianity's seminal contribution to romanticism. He does not suggest that romanticism has a Christian essence, so that his claim is in no way diminished by researches which find the origins of romantic poetry in the courts of Moorish Spain. Hegel's argument is that Christianity made romanticism possible, even in a sense necessary, by introducing a new conception of the soul and of its place in the universe.

If Hegel is correct one might have expected the romanticism of the Romantic Movement to have generated a quickening of religious sensibility. In many cases, as we have seen, it did so. Rousseau himself tells us that his respect for the deity led him to break with the atheists of the Enlightenment, and prompted his return to the Church of Geneva. Chateaubriand, Manzoni, Eichendorff and many more were fortified in their obedience to Catholic discipline as they extended romanticism from a theory of art into a philosophy of life. Others found the free spirit of romanticism better matched by less rigid formulations of Christian doctrine.

After the scepticism and rationalism that was so prevalent in the eighteenth century, the nineteenth century witnessed various forms of religious revival, and it can hardly be denied that the Romantic Movement contributed to this, even though it would seem, with the Rousseauesque doctrine of man's natural goodness, to have stimulated belief in as many alternative creeds, such as Auguste Comte's religion of humanity, as in Christianity itself. The most obvious impact of romanticism beyond the realm of culture in nineteenth-century Europe was, however, political. The much-discussed association of romanticism with revolution has, as we have noted, to be balanced against its association with conservatism. The alliance of romanticism with nationalism is less equivocal. If it is most pronounced in the cases of Germany and Italy, these are by no means the only countries in which the history of the romantic movement is also the history of its nationalism.

Again, it must not be overlooked that the character of such nationalisms varied, for while nationalism can properly be considered an ideology, it is by no means unambiguous. The 'nation' is a much disputed concept, and nationalism has assumed a different form in different contexts: and these differences in turn have had their effect not only on the ideals to which the romantic imagination has been directed, but on the tone and colour of romantic expression.

It is customary to date the emergence of romanticism in Russia from the publication of Fyodor Emin's *Letters of Ernest and Doravra*, which is little more than an adaptation into Russian of *La nouvelle Héloïse*, but this is to suggest an alien origin for a movement which had its roots in Russia's own literary tradition. Russian romanticism can best be seen as developing out of Russian sentimentalism. It was a characteristic of this school of writers to indulge in flights of fancy and what the critic Nikolay Karamyin called 'effusions of emotion' – a cult of feeling for feeling's sake. If this falls short of an authentic romantic commitment to imagination as the agent of truth, there is a clear line of continuity between such sentimentalist poetry and the full flowering of Russian romanticism in the work of Pushkin, who first startled the world at the age of twenty-one with his poem *Ruslan and Liudmila*, based on a Russian folk tale. There is a message of freedom in this poem, and an even more unmistakable one in Pushkin's cycle of lyrics which followed it. Then at the age of thirty-four Pushkin published his masterpiece *Eugene Onegin*, a novel in verse which takes the whole of Russian life as its subject, observing the world with the keen eye of a Balzac while maintaining the spiritual inwardness of a Coleridge.

Pushkin died a romantic death in a duel at the age of thirty-seven. An ode in his memory by Mikhail Lermontov, then a young Guards officer who aspired to be the Byron of Russia, caused almost as much of a sensation as any poem by Pushkin himself, for Lermontov coupled his lament for the poet's death with a denunciation of the noblemen of the court and the imperial despotism they supported. Lermontov was banished to the Caucasus, and although he was allowed to return to St Petersburg within a year, he remained an outspoken champion of freedom, even, at times, of revolution. Like many of the French Romantics, he regarded the July Revolution of 1830 in Paris as a triumph of liberty, and his published attacks on the tyranny of Charles X in France were readily assumed to be equally, if not mainly, directed at the rule of Nicholas I in Russia. History repeated itself in 1841

when Lermontov, aged twenty-seven, died like his hero Pushkin in a duel with a fellow officer.

The Romantic Movement in Russia was reinvigorated by
the musicians, the true heirs of eighteenth-century sentimentalism. Pushkin's writings furnished *libretti* for their operas,
and the composers vied with each other in creating a distinc-
tly Russian, as opposed to a European lyrical theatre. In the
case of Glinka this entailed a conscious repudiation of the
models he had studied as a young man in Italy, and a return
to indigenous folk music for the inspiration of such operas as
A Life of the Czar and *Ruslan and Liudmila*, based on Pushkin's
poem. Borodin, Mussorgsky and Rimsky-Korsakov demonstrated their 'Russianness' and commitment to a national
form of music by keeping well away from the conservatories
and the westernized professors, so that they were largely
self-taught. If Tchaikovsky was more cosmopolitan in his
sympathies, his romanticism carried within it the most un-
diluted infusion of the old sentimentalism.

The nationalism of Russian romanticism thus took the
form of asserting Russia's unique identity and character, the
'Russianness' of Russian art, and it was to this extent, conservative. In Poland romantic art was more revolutionary. The
Poles did badly out of the carve-up of Europe at the Congress
of Vienna in 1815, and worse as both the Russian and Prussian rulers proceeded to rob them of what little freedom
remained to them. Romantic art in these circumstances became the voice of national protest and resistance. The aim of
nationalism in nineteenth-century Poland was rather different from that of nationalism in Italy, where its mission was
the creation of a cultural nation, or in Germany, where it
sought to transform a cultural nation into a political nation.
Poland already had its history as a political nation, united
under its kings, and the programme of its nationalists was
simple: to dismiss the alien intruder and restore what had
been lost. The romantic poets of Poland had no motive for

digging into ancient folklore to rekindle national consciousness or to purify and energize the Polish language to express
a finer literature; the popular consciousness and the linguistic
resources were already there. Adam Michiewicz, whose first
book was published in 1822, was acknowledged to be the
greatest poet of the Polish Romantic Movement, an urbane
and sophisticated versifier. At the same time his plea for
liberty was so eloquent that the occupying power could not
ignore it, and after his second book of poems appeared in
1823 he was banished to a life of exile. But, even in Switzerland and France, Michiewicz produced writings which circu-
lated in Poland and kept alive faith in the ultimate liberation
of the kingdom. The Polish insurrections of 1830, 1846 and
1863 could hardly have been expected to overthrow the
regime, but Michiewicz and Chopin and dozens of lesser
writers and musicians inspired the Polish people to act on
romantic hopes rather than rational calculations of probable
success.

In Scandinavia the situation was more complicated. In
Iceland and Norway romanticism was allied with political
movements, whereas in Sweden and Denmark it was more
purely cultural. This difference reflects a difference in the
political situation of the four countries at that stage in history; Norway was under Swedish rule, Iceland under Danish;
and moreover in the case of Norway, Swedish political control
was coupled with Danish cultural hegemony. This explains
Norwegian and Icelandic yearnings for national liberation.
The Norwegian poet Henrik Wergeland published in 1830
an epic entitled *Creation, Humanity and Messiah* which served
as a manifesto of 'national romanticism'. Its impact was reinforced by the publication in the following years of large
collections of *Norwegian Folk Tales* by Asbjørnsen and Moe
and *Norwegian Folk Ballads* by Magnus Landstad. The purpose of all these enterprises was to assert Norway's claim to
recognition as an independent cultural entity distinct from

that of a mere Scandinavian province. Romanticism doubtless contributed much towards the restoration of the Norwegian kingdom which was achieved fairly peacefully in 1905. In Iceland the Romantic Movement generated what was in effect a cultural renaissance, with poets such as Egilsson, Thorarensen, Hallgrimsson, Gröndal and others emerging from a tiny population to provide some of the finest Scandinavian lyrics and epic poems on the theme of liberty.

In the New World, romanticism could claim, with good reason, to have animated the nationalist rebellions which led to the liberation of the peoples of Latin America from the sovereignty of Spain and Portugal. These events occurred during the heyday of the Romantic Movement in the early nineteenth century. Simón Bolivar, remembered as '*El Libertador*', is as splendid a model of the romantic hero as any European, a more effective soldier than Byron and a more genuine champion of freedom than Napoleon. It is said of him that after reading the works of Montesquieu and Rousseau, he stood on the summit of Monte Sacro in Rome and took an oath to liberate his country – his country being not only Colombia (as it is now called) where he was born, but also Venezuela, Ecuador, Bolivia and Peru. This romantic gesture led soon to action. Early successes were followed by defeats and exile; then in exile Bolivar produced a manifesto *La Carta de Jamaica*, which inspired a whole generation with its vision of Latin America, from the northern border of Mexico down to the southern tip of Chile, from which all European power was banished and the people ruled themselves in free autonomous republics. Bolivar's ideas were echoed in verse by the Cuban Heredia y Heredia, Latin America's first great lyric poet, in prose by its first novelist the Mexican Lizardi; and by a whole group of Argentinian writers around Echeverria and Sarmiento who produced in the Spanish language poems with nothing of Spain in them, but possessing distinctively Latin-American qualities of colour and rhythm.

Brazilian poets had been engaged at an even earlier stage in the movement for national liberation, and when independence finally came in 1822 a romantic poet Andrada e Silva was hailed as the patriarch of the new autonomous empire.

Romanticism had no such role in the events which led to the independence of the United States, nor any such prominence in the early years of the nation which independence brought into being. The North American revolution, coming so many years earlier than the several Latin American dramas of rebellion, belonged to another era.

The United States was too much the creature of the Enlightenment, its culture too profoundly shaped by eighteenth-century rationalism and empiricism for romanticism to be readily appreciated there. Besides, the American commitment to the ideal of a republican society prompted its citizens to respond to the austere maxims of ancient Rome rather than the enchantments of medieval feudal Christendom. The powerful Puritan tradition was inimical to free flights of the imagination. Ralph Waldo Emerson was able to make romanticism a significant presence in nineteenth-century American culture only by expressing it in the elevated form he called transcendentalism. Emerson started out as a Unitarian preacher, only to be impelled by religious doubts to make a close study of the then fashionable European authors, especially the German critics and philosophers recommended in *De l'Allemagne* by Mme de Staël. He later turned to Hegel and also made the personal acquaintance in England of Coleridge and Carlyle. In 1836, at the age of thirty-three, he published an essay entitled *Nature* which endures as the first manifesto of American romanticism, a work of lofty eloquence in which the author suggests that since God is within each of us, the highest purpose of life must be to explore one's own inwardness. He also argues that since there is 'a correspondence between the human soul and everything that exists in the world' the pursuit of introspective reveries is an exercise in search of truth and therefore noble.

Romanticism also arrived in America in a devious way through the influence of popular literature on serious literature. Two events furthered this process. The first was the Civil War, which stimulated a number of novelists, such as Stephen Crane whose *Red Badge of Courage* reached out to a mass public with a story which was largely about the inward experience of combat. The second event was the opening of the West, which produced a new genre of 'cowboy fiction' which, well before its exploitation in the cinema, represented an important and totally American contribution to romantic art. This genre had something in common with the *gaucho* literature produced in Argentina and Uruguay a generation earlier, at least to the extent that its heroes were cowboys and its location the wild interior; but whereas the Latin Americans were at their best in writing ballads, the North Americans excelled as novelists.

Strangely, the titles of those Western stories – *The Virginians*, *Shane* and *High Noon*, for example – are better remembered than the names of Western writers such as Owen Wister, A. B. Guthrie and Walter van Tilburg Clark. Owen Wister, perhaps the best of the group, a man of high culture, who had studied classics at Harvard and music in Paris, was fully conscious of the Rousseauesque elements in his fiction: the exaltation of nature in its pristine form that the pioneers discovered at the frontier together with a melancholy sense that their very arrival would soon destroy the wildness of the nature they loved. Owen Wister also gave the Western novel its standard plot: the ill-fated love of the rough cowboy hero for a better-educated heroine from the East, St-Preux and Julie *redivivus*.

Those novels belong to the last years of the nineteenth century. In Europe by that time, the Romantic Movement, and the intense high form of romanticism associated with it, was on the wane. The word 'romantic' came to be associated with what was no longer fashionable. As the century approached its end, new movements which called themselves 'realist', 'naturalist', 'symbolist' or 'formalist' took command of the cultural avant-garde, proclaiming their dissent from the ideas of Rousseau and *die romantische Schule*. At the same time efforts were made to assimilate romanticism into more comprehensive systems. The most ambitious of these was Hegel's own. He developed a form of idealism which could be said to have effected a reconciliation of romanticism and rationalism. In the dialectical logic which Hegel introduced, contradictions, conflicts, tensions, obscurities, intuitions and intimations – all the proceedings of the romantic mind that are anathema to Cartesian philosophy – are accepted rather than avoided because Hegel maintains that competition in thought, as in economic life, furthers progress and that the clash of antitheses can yield a synthesis. His objective idealism thus offers access for romantic notions of spontaneity and imagination into the framework of a total rational system.

Another philosopher – and one who was not at all sympathetic to Hegel's logic – also sought to incorporate romantic elements into his rationalism. This was John Stuart Mill, who tells us in his *Autobiography* of 1873 how, after being brought up in the dry principles of eighteenth-century empiricism, he discovered the poetry of Wordsworth at the age of twenty, and thereafter sought to promote a fusion between the analytic and utilitarian methods of the Enlightenment with 'the cultivation of feelings'. This objective became henceforth 'one of the cardinal points in my ethical and philosophical creed.' In his theory of individual liberty, Mill adopted Diderot's notion of freedom as self-realization, an activity which, as he explained, was bound to put men at odds with the oppressive tendencies of conventional society and find its best expression in the life-style of the eccentric, the outsider, the Bohemian. Mill's liberalism was a romantic liberalism, and therein lay its originality.

In music in the middle of the nineteenth century, Richard Wagner attempted another synthesis: that of romanticism with classicism. By 1848 virtually all European music was romantic music, and it was immensely popular. Wagner attributed its popularity to its having come to embody the values of bourgeois society and to furnish that society with what he declared to be mere 'entertainment'. This attack was directed in particular at opera, and Wagner proclaimed his intention to banish opera as it was known and replace it with a 'music theatre' modelled on the drama of classical antiquity, a theatre which, like the tragedies of Greece, would unite the arts of poetry, drama, dance, mime, scenery and song in a total performance. He would bring audiences together in assemblies of rich religious significance, as in a temple or church. Wagner saw himself as recovering a truly classical model for the future of music in general and for his own operas in particular. It may be questioned whether the operas Wagner composed fulfil the aims set out in his theoretical writings, for the barbaric passions and the pagan religiosity they express seem far removed from classical ideals, but there is no denying their splendour and originality, or their capacity to evoke, in those who most appreciate them, an ecstatic, devotional response. If they transcend romanticism, they also carry it to extremes.

Wagner's complaint about romantic art having become by 1848 'bourgeois' is one that is commonly heard. Yet it is not easy to reconcile it with the criticism addressed to the poets of the Jena and the Heidelberg schools, to Chateaubriand, Hugo and Vigny, that their romanticism expressed the yearnings of a dispossessed nobility for a lost world of chivalry. Nor does it fit Mill's image of romantic liberty at odds with middle-class morality; or with the Bohemian character of the romantic personality as exemplified by Shelley and Byron and copied by innumerable young artists, writers, and students in their garrets.

Nevertheless Wagner did not wholly misrepresent the situation. By 1848, and indeed even earlier, romanticism had assumed more than one form – the radical, subversive form it had for Rousseau and his followers, and the consoling form that Walter Scott gave it. The kind of romanticism which Wagner condemned as 'entertainment' was of the consoling kind, and in the hands of Walter Scott's successors, such as Dickens and many men of lesser genius, romanticism was discreetly softened into sentimentalism.

Romanticism thus diminished in what came to dominate bourgeois culture in the second half of the nineteenth century, especially in Germany and Great Britain. It is everything suggested by the word 'Victorian'. Its manifestations include the Gothic revival in architecture, which symbolized, and indeed accommodated, a revival in church attendance and worship. Its poetry – as the Tennysons and Austins succeeded the Shelleys and Keats – exalted purity in thought and deed. Its paintings, especially those of the Pre-Raphaelite school, veiled erotic subjects in biblical clothing, and helped to sublimate the sexual. The prophets of Victorianized romanticism – Ruskin, William Morris and Matthew Arnold – were no longer cantankerous critics like Carlyle, cursing money and mines and factories, but practical reformers providing workshops and studios in which labour could recover the lost dignity of the craftsman. Even the greatest of all Victorian projects, the rebuilding of the Empire, was reinforced by its own kind of romanticism, proclaiming the excitement of the unknown, the charm of exploration and the thrill of adventure overseas as an escape from Blake's dark Satanic mills. In Germany, compulsory service in the army was rendered glamorous by equally seductive appeals to the imagination, and romance was introduced into the dull grind of university study by opportunities for that most chivalrous of exercises, duelling.

It was partly by reason of this association with the sentimental and a somewhat meritricious 'idealism', that romanticism became suspect in certain circles in the later part of the nineteenth century. In the movement of the positivistic *Zeitgeist*, several writers and critics attempted to give art an empirical status. Zola's novels are perhaps an extreme case of this endeavour to base literature on the external factual observation of human behaviour as opposed to imaginative insight into human experience. A more moderate plea for naturalism was made by the Spanish-born American critic George Santayana in his book *The Sense of Beauty* of 1896 where he put forward a 'scientific' theory of aesthetics, denying art any more ideal quality than that of 'objectified pleasure'. In his later writings on art, however, Santayana discarded his early naturalism in favour of a theory which gave high priority to the faculty of imagination. Indeed he went so far as to suggest that the 'life of reason' is itself a 'life of the imagination' in which a 'process of idealization and symbolic transformation provides the richest elements in mental experience'. Santayana in effect came to adopt something close to the romantic metaphysics of Coleridge.

Another American exponent of naturalism was John Dewey, who was more noted in his earlier years for his attempt to reconstruct the concept of experience in the light of the experimental method of the sciences. But when he produced in 1934 a treatise on aesthetics called *Art as Experience* he, too, was discovered to have much in common with the philosophy of romanticism.

Other theorists were more radical in their posture. In the early years of the present century, some of the most influential and fashionable writers mounted a sustained campaign for a 'return to classicism'. Charles Maurras in France, T. E. Hulme in England and Irving Babbitt in America produced vigorous attacks on Rousseau, scornful appraisals of the work of Victor Hugo, Wordsworth, Shelley, Dumas and the rest of the Romantics, while pointing to Racine and Corneille and the metaphysical poets of the seventeenth century as the only modern authors affording decent models of order, discipline and aesthetic decorum. Although this demand for a counter-revolution against romanticism came from the Right, it commanded the adherence of some of the most advanced writers and artists of the earlier twentieth century: among them Ezra Pound, T. S. Eliot, Paul Claudel, Paul Valéry, the imagists, the vorticists and many more. Modernists were called upon to return to classicism. Even those innovators in music, art and architecture who resisted that call were at any rate emphatic in asserting that they were *not* romantic.

However, this counter-revolution proved less successful than its champions believed. In a book with the apt title of *The Romantic Survival*, Professor John Bayley pointed out in the 1950s that the new 'classical' school of English poetry represented by T. S. Eliot, T. E. Hulme and Ezra Pound had been followed by another group of poets, including W. B. Yeats, W. H. Auden and Dylan Thomas whose work is unmistakably romantic. What Professor Bayley says of English poetry could be said of most other manifestations of western twentieth-century art. Despite pleas for the 'classical' by Gabriel Fauré and other leading teachers of composition in the early twentieth-century, virtually all the greatest composers since that time – Mahler, Shostakovich, Britten and the rest – have kept alive the romantic tradition. The novel, which is almost by definition romantic, has resisted all the endeavours of 'experimental' writers such as Joyce and Beckett and Butor, to revolutionize what Henry James called 'the fictive art'. In America, where romanticism was regarded so coolly by the Founders and the Puritans, various forms of romanticism have been cultivated with enthusiasm by their liberated twentieth-century descendants. No amount of official demands for social realism in the Soviet Union could quell the romanticism of Pasternak and Akhmatova.

In Hegel's philosophy of art, romanticism could not have been extinguished by a 'classical counter-revolution' or by 'social realism' or by any other entirely new mode of art, on the grounds that romantic art marks the terminal phase. According to the Hegelian scheme, symbolic art represents the thesis, classical art the antithesis, and romantic art represents the synthesis, in which art achieves its perfection. Beyond this art has nowhere further to go.

It is a bold claim, based on Hegel's theory that the unfolding of history is dialectical, and the purpose of art the revelation of the eternal in sensible form. The theory may be questioned, but time cannot be said to have refuted the assertion, for while the golden age of the Romantic Movement ended in the nineteenth century, romanticism in Hegel's broad sense of the word, has outlived the opposition and the counter-revolution, and still informs a large part of what is most modern and contemporary in art, philosophy and literature.

Selected Bibliography of Critical Works

General

Abrams, Mark, *The Mirror and the Lamp*, Oxford, Oxford University Press, 1953

Abrams, Mark, *Natural Supernaturalism*, New York, W. W. Norton and Co., 1972

Barzun, Jacques, *Romanticism and the Modern Ego*, Boston, Little Brown and Co., 1944

Barzun, Jacques, *Classic, Romantic and Modern*, London, Secker and Warburg, 1962

Bate, Walter Jackson, *From Classic to Romantic*, Cambridge, Cambridge University Press, 1946

Bloom, Harold, (Ed.), *Romanticism and Consciousness*, New York, W. W. Norton and Co., 1970

Bornstein, George, (Ed.), *Romantic and Modern*, Pittsburgh, Pittsburgh University Press, 1977

Clark, Kenneth, *The Gothic Revival*, New York, Scribners, 1950

Cooke, Michael, *The Romantic Will*, New Haven, Yale University Press, 1976

Davies, R. T. and Beaty, R. G., *Literature of the Romantic Period*, Liverpool, Liverpool University Press, 1976

Driver, Tom, *Romantic Quest and Modern Query*, New York, Delacorte Press, 1970

Ehrmann, Jacques, (Ed.), *Literature and Revolution*, Boston, Beacon Press, 1970

Furst, Lillian R., *The Contours of European Romanticism*, Lincoln, University of Nebraska Press, 1979

Halsted, J. B., *Romanticism*, Boston, Heath and Co., 1965

Hegel, G. W. F., *Philosophy of Fine Art*, four vols, London, G. Bell and Sons, 1920

Heller, Erich, *The Artist's Journey into the Interior*, London, Secker and Warburg, 1966

Kaufmann, Walter, *Tragedy and Philosophy*, New York, Doubleday, 1969

Kermode, Frank, *The Romantic Image*, London, Collins, 1957

Krook, Dorothea, *Elements of Tragedy*, New Haven, Yale University Press, 1969

Nemoianu, Virgil, *The Taming of Romanticism*, Cambridge, Mass., Harvard University Press, 1984

Peyre, Henri, *What is Romanticism?*, Alabama, Alabama University Press, 1977

Simpson, David, *Irony and Authority in Romantic Poetry*, London, Macmillan, 1979

Steiner, George, *The Death of Tragedy*, London, Faber and Faber, 1961

Thorlby, Anthony, *The Romantic Movement*, London, Longmans, 1966

Wellek, R., *A History of Modern Criticism: The Romantic Age*, New Haven, Yale University Press, 1955

German Romanticism

Boyle, Nicholas, *Goethe*, Oxford, Oxford University Press, 1991

Brandes, Georges, *Main Currents in Modern Literature*, vol. II, London, Macmillan, 1902

Carlson, Marvin, *The German Stage in the Nineteenth Century*, Metuchen, NJ, Scarecrow Press, 1972

Eichner, Hans, *Friedrich Schlegel*, New York, Twayne, 1970

Garland, H. B., *Storm and Stress*, London, Harrap, 1952

Grimm, R., (Ed.), *Romanticism Today*, Bonn, Zeitschrift für deutsche Philologie, 1973

Hamburger, Michael, *Contraries: Studies in German Literature*, London, Weidenfeld and Nicolson, 1970

Hayman, Ronald, (Ed.), *The German Theatre*, New York, Barnes and Noble, 1975

Heitner, R. R., *German Tragedy in the Age of Enlightenment*, Berkeley, University of California Press, 1963

Heller, Erich, *In the Age of Prose*, Cambridge, Cambridge University Press, 1984

Hughes, Glyn Tegai, *Romantic German Literature: 1760–1805*, New York, Holmes and Meier, 1975

Lukacs, Georg, *Goethe and his Age*, New York, Grosset and Dunlap, 1969

Magee, Bryan, *Aspects of Wagner*, Oxford, Oxford University Press, 1970

Pascal, Roy, *The German Sturm und Drang*, Manchester, Manchester University Press, 1953

Prawer, Siegbert, *The Romantic Period in Germany*, New York, Schocken Books, 1970

Reiss, H., (Ed.), *The Political Thought of the German Romantics*, Oxford, Oxford University Press, 1955

Robertson, J. G., *A History of German Literature*, Edinburgh, William Blackwood and Sons, 1959

Willoughby, L. A., *The Romantic Movement in Germany*, Oxford, Oxford University Press, 1930

Ziolkowski, Theodore, *German Romanticism and its Institutions*, Princeton, Princeton University Press, 1990

English Romanticism

Ball, Patricia M., *The Central Self*, London, Athlone Press, 1968

Bayley, John, *The Romantic Survival*, Oxford, Oxford University Press, 1957

Bowra, C. M., *The Romantic Imagination*, Oxford, Oxford University Press, 1950

Brinton, Crane, *The Political Ideas of the English Romanticists*, Ann Arbor, University of Michigan Press, 1962

Butler, Marilyn, *Romantics, Rebels and Reactionaries*, Oxford, Oxford University Press, 1981

Clubbe, John and Lovell, E. J., *English Romanticism*, Champaign, University of Illinois Press, 1983

Cobban, Alfred, *Edmund Burke and the Revolt Against the Eighteenth Century*, New York, Barnes and Noble, 1939

Fletcher, Richard, *English Romantic Drama*, New York, Exposition Press, 1966

Foakes, R. A., *The Romantic Assertion*, London, Methuen, 1958

Frye, Northrop, *A Study of English Romanticism*, New York, Random House, 1968

Gaull, Marilyn, *English Romanticism*, New York, W. W. Norton and Co., 1983

Jones, J., *The Egotistical Sublime*, Oxford, Oxford University Press, 1954

Kettle, Arnold, *Introduction to the English Novel*, London, Hutchinson, 1951

Murry, Middleton John, *Keats and Shakespeare*, London, Jonathan Cape, 1934

Read, Herbert, *The True Voice of Feeling*, London, Routledge, 1953

Woodring, Carl, *Politics in English Romantic Poetry*, Cambridge, Mass., Harvard University Press, 1970

French Romanticism

Adam, Antoine, *Grandeur and Illusion: French Literature and Society*, London, Weidenfeld and Nicolson, 1972

de Bertier de Sauvigny, G., *The Bourbon Restoration*, Philadelphia, Pennsylvania University Press, 1968

Carlson, Marvin, *The French Stage in the Nineteenth Century*, Metuchen, NJ, Scarecrow Press, 1972

Charlton, D. C., (Ed.), *The French Romantics*, two vols, Cambridge, Cambridge University Press, 1984

Denommé, Robert, *Nineteenth-Century French Romantic Poets*, Carbondale, Ill., Southern Illinois University Press, 1969

Draper, F. W. M., *The Rise and Fall of French Romantic Drama*, London, Constable, 1923

Hartman, Elwood, *French Romantics on Progress*, Madrid, Studia Humanitatis, 1983

Howarth, W. D., *Sublime and Grotesque, a Study of French Romantic Drama*, London, Harrap, 1975

Matthews, Brander, *French Dramatists of the Nineteenth Century*, New York, Scribners, 1905

Nicolson, Harold, *Sainte-Beuve*, London, Constable, 1954

Ridge, George Ross, *The Hero in French Romantic Literature*, Athens, GA, University of Georgia Press, 1959

Schamber, Ellie Nower, *The Artist as Politician: The Art and Politics of the French Romantics*, New York, University Press of America, 1984

Schroder, Maurice, *Icarus: The Image of the Artist in French Romanticism*, Cambridge, Mass., Harvard University Press, 1961

Starobinski, Jean, *The Emblems of Reason*, Charlottesville, University of Virginia Press, 1982

Italian Romanticism

Avitabile, Grazia, *The Controversy on Romanticism in Italy*, New York, Vanni Inc., 1959

Barricelli, Jean-Pierre, *Alessandro Manzoni*, Boston, Twayne, 1976

Cairns, Christopher, *Italian Literature: The Dominant Themes*, Newton Abbott, David and Charles, 1977

Chandler, S. B., *Alessandro Manzoni*, Edinburgh, Edinburgh University Press, 1974

Perella, Nicolas J., *Night and the Sublime in Giacomo Leopardi*, Berkeley, University of California Press, 1970

Verhoeven, Cornalis, *The Philosophy of Wonder*, New York, Macmillan, 1972

Vincent, E. R., *Ugo Foscolo*, Cambridge, Cambridge University Press, 1953

Whitfield, J. H., *Leopardi*, Oxford, Oxford University Press, 1954

Whitfield, J. H., *A History of Italian Literature*, London, Cassell, 1962

Wilkins, E. H., *A History of Italian Literature*, Cambridge, Mass., Harvard University Press, 1974

Spanish Romanticism

Brenan, Gerald, *The Literature of the Spanish People*, Cambridge, Cambridge University Press, 1953

Chandler, Richard and Schwarz, Kessel, *A New History of Spanish Literature*, Baton Rouge, Louisiana State University Press, 1961

Deyermond, A. D., *A Literary History of the Spanish Middle Ages*, London, Ernest Benn, 1971

Glendenning, Nigel, *A Literary History of Spain: The Eighteenth Century*, London, Ernest Benn, 1972

Green, Otis H., *Spain and the Western Tradition*, four vols, Madison, University of Wisconsin Press, 1966

Jones, R. O., (Ed.), *A Literary History of Spain: The Golden Age*, London, Ernest Benn, 1971

Kirkpatrick, Susan, *Las Romanticas: Women Writers in Spain*, Berkeley, University of California Press, 1989

Parker, Alexander, *The Philosophy of Love in Spanish Literature*, Edinburgh, Edinburgh University Press, 1935

Peers, E. Allison, *History of the Romantic Movement in Spain*, two vols, Cambridge, Cambridge University Press, 1940

Shaw, Donald L., *A Literary History of Spain: The Nineteenth Century*, London, Ernest Benn, 1972

Sommer, Doris, *Foundational Fiction*, Berkeley, University of California Press, 1991

Terry, Arthur, *Catalan Literature*, London, Ernest Benn, 1972

Thomas, Henry, *Spanish and Portuguese Romances of Chivalry*, Cambridge, Cambridge University Press, 1928

Index